The Ultimate Hedge Fund Guide

Frank Nagy

Published by CreateSpace Independent Publishing

No part of this publication may be reproduced, stored or transmitted in any form or means, electronic, scan, photocopying, or otherwise permitted, without the express written permission of the Publisher.

Disclaimer: The Publisher and Author make no representations or warranties with respect to the accuracy or completeness of the contents of this book. The advice, strategies, and structures contained in this book may not be suitable for all situations or persons. Neither the Publisher nor Author shall be liable for any loss of profit, or any other commercial damages.

ANY SERVICES OFFERED, OPINIONS, NEWS, ANALYSES OR OTHER INFORMATION CONTAINED IN THIS BOOK IS PROVIDED AS GENERAL INFORMATION AND DOES NOT CONSTITUTE INVESTMENT, LEGAL OR TAX ADVICE OR SOLICITATION OF SUCH SERVICES. FRANK NAGY OR FRANK NAGY FINANCIAL SERVICES DOES NOT OFFER OR SELL SECURITIES.

The Ultimate Hedge Fund Guide – First Edition

Copyright © 2014 by Frank Nagy

All rights reserved.

ISBN-13:978-1503134973
ISBN-10:1503134970

CONTENTS

PREFACE 1

WHO REGULATES "WHAT" 2
    SECURITIES ACT OF 1933..3
    THE INVESTMENT COMPANY ACT OF 1940 3
    THE INVESTMENT ADVISERS ACT OF 1940 3
    SARBANES-OXLEY ACT OF 2002 4
    DODD-FRANK WALL STREET REFORM ACT 4
    EXEMPTIONS FOR ADVISERS TO VENTURE CAPITAL FUNDS, ADVISERS WITH LESS THAN $150 MILLION IN ASSETS UNDER MANAGEMENT, AND FOREIGN PRIVATE ADVISERS 5
    THE INVESTMENT ADVISERS ACT INVESTOR CRITERIA............................7
    U.S. COMMODITY FUTURES TRADING COMMISSION............................10
    THE EUROPEAN UNION ALTERNATIVE INVESTMENT FUND MANAGERS DIRECTIVE (AIFMD) 11

SELECTING YOUR INVESTMENT STYLE & STRATEGY 13
    EMERGING MARKET 14
    EQUITY DIRECTIONAL...14
    EQUITY MARKET NEUTRAL 15
    EVENT DRIVEN...16
    FIXED INCOME DIRECTIONAL 17
    FIXED INCOME RELATIVE VALUE 17
    MANAGED FUTURES/CTA..18
    GLOBAL MACRO 19
    MULTI-STRATEGY/MULTI-STYLE..19

HOW MUCH ARE YOU WORTH?..20
    MANAGEMENT FEES 20
    PERFORMANCE FEES..21
    OTHER FEES AND EXPENSES 23

PUTTING IT ALL TOGETHER: SETTING THE RULES FOR MANAGING YOUR FUND 25
    CAPITAL CONTRIBUTIONS..25
    COMPLIANCE 27
    LIST OF INVESTOR KYC DOCUMENTS...30
    FROM SUBSCRIBER TO INVESTOR 31

UNDERSTANDING YOUR OFFERING DOCUMENTS 32
PRIVATE PLACEMENT MEMORANDUM 32
The Summary 33
Directory 37
Introduction 37
Investment Activities of the Fund 40
Management Company of the Fund 40
Administrator 41
Auditor 43
Valuation of the Fund's Assets 43
Anti-Money Laundering Considerations 44
Certain Income Tax Considerations 45
Securities Laws 46
Reports to Partners (Investors) 47
Subscriptions Procedures 47
Risk Factors 47
SUBSCRIPTION AGREEMENT 50
Subscription Agreement Terms and Declarations 51
Accredited Investor Certification 55
Individuals (Questionnaire) 55
Entities (Questionnaire) 56
Wire Transfer Page 58
Signature Page 58
LIMITED PARTNERSHIP AGREEMENT 58

CHOOSING THE RIGHT ENTITY STRUCTURE 60
Liability 60
Formalities 61
Filing Costs 61
Delaware Limited Partnership 61
Delaware Formation Process 62
Delaware Formalities 62
U.S. or Offshore Investors 63
Offshore Fund – Ltd 63
BVI Closed-end Fund 63
BVI Professional Fund 64
FUND STRUCTURE 64

ASSEMBLING YOUR "A" TEAM 66

Your Attorney	67
Your Administrator	68
Your Auditor	69
Your Banker	70
Your Prime Broker	72

DISASTER RECOVERY & BUSINESS CONTINUITY PLANNING 74

Disaster Recovery Planning	75
Business Continuity Planning	75
Developing an Operations Manual	76

GET READY TO LAUNCH 78

Raising Capital	78
Developing a Plan to Attract Investors	78
Seed yourself	*78*
Seed investors	*79*
High-net-worth individuals	*79*
Family offices	*79*
Institutional investors	*80*
Marketing Your Fund	82
Publish a press release	*82*
Speak at public events	*82*
Write a book	*82*
Create a pitch book	*82*
Market to small wealth managers	*82*
Legal Items to Consider	83
Beware of Unlicensed Introducing Agents	*84*
Issuer's "Exemption" and Associated Persons of Issuers (Rule 3a4-1)	*84*
Marketing your Hedge Fund in the European Union	*84*

A FINAL WORD 86
GLOSSARY 87
REFERENCES 103
INDEX 104
ABOUT THE AUTHOR 107

PREFACE

The history of hedge funds dates back as early as 1949. The founder of the very first hedge fund was Alfred Jones. A financial journalist by profession, Mr. Jones started the first hedge fund in 1949. His belief was that if he could buy a specific asset that would expect to appreciate in the future while selling short assets whose price he expected to decrease. And thus creating a neutralizing effect of the overall market movement. By taking this investment approach his investment strategy was described as "market neutral." Jones referred to his portfolio as being "hedged" to describe how a fund managed risk exposure from overall market movement. This particular portfolio became known as a hedge fund.

By 1952, Mr. Jones decided to convert his fund into a limited partnership and charge a performance fee of 20%. He became the very first money manager to combine hedging strategies while utilizing leverage. Brilliant you might say? It sure was back then.

From that point on, hedge funds became the talk of the town. By 1968 there were over 200 hedge funds. From 1970 hedge funds typically specialized only in one strategy, and most fund managers followed the long/short trading model created by its founder Jones. Then at some point, hedge funds lost their thrill but in the late 1980s following the success of several funds profiled in the media the industry picked right back up.

Over the next two decade, there were new techniques of diversification in the funds utilized. This included: quantitative, distressed debt, credit arbitrage, multi-strategy as well as fixed income.

1
WHO REGULATES "WHAT"

All hedge funds have some type of regulations which they must adhere to in order for them to operate. From federal laws to state laws to regulations that govern funds in Europe and beyond, the fund manager/sponsor is responsible to navigate through these various rules so that he does not get in hot water. Thankfully, you can rely on the competence and experience of your securities attorney. Who, by the way, should be up to speed on all the current rules and regs.

The Securities and Exchange Commission (SEC) is an independent federal agency that is responsible for adopting and enforcing federal laws that regulate the securities market. Markets include the U.S. stock exchanges, options market as well as the electronic securities market.

The primary regulations that the SEC enforces are the Securities Act of 1933, the Securities Exchange Act of 1934, the Investment Company Act of 1940, the Investment Advisers Act of 1940, the Sarbanes-Oxley Act of 2002, the Dodd-Frank Act, and other statutes. For commodities, futures, and options on futures, there is another division that is called the Commodity Futures Trading Commission. The Commodity Futures Trading Commission (CFTC) is an independent federal agency that regulates, together with the SEC, many aspects of the derivatives market. Both governing bodies are there to protect market users and the public from fraud, manipulation, and abusive practices in the sale of commodity and financial futures and options, and to foster open, competitive option markets.

To understand how your hedge fund will be looked upon by the regulators, you must first understand what the Securities Act of 1933 (The Act) is. The Act contains rules and provisions that provide protection for investors. The Act requires that all publicly offered securities be registered. The Act also provides limited exemptions for certain offerings, including private offerings to a limited number of sophisticated persons or institutions; offerings of limited size; intrastate offerings; and securities of municipal, state, and federal governments. This is where your startup hedge fund can rely on certain exemptions which would enable you to raise capital and operate your fund without the need for registration with the SEC. But we'll talk about that later. The following is described by the SEC:

Securities Act of 1933: Only accredited investors can invest in hedge funds. Accredited investors include individuals who have a minimum net worth of $1,000,000 or, alternatively, a minimum income of $200,000 in each of the last two years and a reasonable expectation of reaching the same income level in the current year. For institutional investors, the minimum net worth is $5,000,000 in invested assets. Hedge funds that have more than 499 investors must register with the SEC and must comply with the quarterly reporting requirement.

The Investment Company Act of 1940: This Act regulates the organization of companies, including mutual funds, that engage primarily in investing, reinvesting, and trading in securities, and whose own securities are offered to the investing public. The regulation is designed to minimize conflicts of interest that arise in these complex operations. The Act requires these companies to disclose their financial condition and investment policies to investors when stock is initially sold and, subsequently, on a regular basis. The focus of this Act is on disclosure to the investing public of information about the fund and its investment objectives, as well as on investment company structure and operations. It is important to remember that the Act does not permit the SEC to directly supervise the investment decisions or activities of these companies or judge the merits of their investments.

The Investment Advisers Act of 1940: This law regulates investment advisers. With certain exceptions, this Act requires that firms or sole practitioners compensated for advising others about securities investments must register with the SEC and conform to regulations designed to protect investors. Since the Act was amended in 1996 and 2010, generally only advisers who have at least $100 million of assets under management or advise a registered investment company must register with the Commission.

Sarbanes-Oxley Act of 2002: On July 30, 2002, President Bush signed into law the Sarbanes-Oxley Act of 2002, which he characterized as "the most far-reaching reforms of American business practices since the time of Franklin Delano Roosevelt." The Act mandated a number of reforms to enhance corporate responsibility, enhance financial disclosures and combat corporate and accounting fraud, and created the "Public Company Accounting Oversight Board," also known as the PCAOB, to oversee the activities of the auditing profession.

Dodd-Frank Wall Street Reform Act: The Dodd-Frank Wall Street Reform and Consumer Protection Act of 2010 was signed into law on July 21, 2010, by President Barack Obama. The legislation set out to reshape the U.S. regulatory system in a number of areas including but not limited to consumer protection, trading restrictions, credit ratings, regulation of financial products, corporate governance and disclosure, and transparency.

However, there are a handful of exemptions that can be relied upon to avoid registering as an investment adviser. According to the SEC, many private fund advisers will be required to register, some of those advisers may not need to if they are able to rely on one of three new exemptions from registration under the Dodd-Frank Act, including exemptions for:

- Advisers solely to venture capital funds.
- Advisers solely to private funds with less than $150 million in assets under management in the U.S.
- Certain foreign advisers without a place of business in the U.S.

The SEC can still impose certain reporting requirements upon advisers relying upon either of the first two of these exemptions ("exempt reporting advisers"). Under the new rules, exempt reporting advisers will nonetheless be required to file, and periodically update, reports with the Commission, using the same registration form as registered advisers.

Rather than completing all of the items on the form, exempt reporting advisers will fill out a limited subset of items, including:

- Basic identifying information for the adviser and the identity of its owners and affiliates.
- Information about the private funds the adviser manages and about other business activities that the adviser and its affiliates are engaged in that present conflicts of interest that may suggest a significant risk to clients.
- The disciplinary history (if any) of the adviser and its employees that may reflect on the integrity of the firm. Exempt reporting advisers will file reports on the Commission's investment adviser electronic filing system (IARD), and these reports will be publicly available on the Commission's website. These advisers will be required to file their first reports in the first quarter of 2012.

The Dodd-Frank Act raises the threshold for Commission registration to $100 million by creating a new category of advisers called "mid-sized advisers." A mid-sized adviser, which generally may not register with the Commission and will be subject to state registration, is defined as an adviser that:

- Manages between $25 million and $100 million for its clients.
- Is required to be registered in the state where it maintains its principal office and place of business.
- Would be subject to examination by that state, if required to register.

Exemptions for Advisers to Venture Capital Funds, Advisers With Less Than $150 Million in Assets Under Management, and Foreign Private Advisers

Advisers to Venture Capital Funds. The Dodd-Frank Act amended the Advisers Act to exempt from registration advisers that only manage venture capital funds, and directed the Commission to define the term "venture capital fund." The SEC further defines Venture capital fund as a fund that:

- Invests primarily in "qualifying investments" (generally, private, operating companies that do not distribute proceeds from debt financings in exchange for the fund's investment in the company); may invest in a "basket" of non-qualifying investments of up to 20 percent of its committed capital; and may hold certain short-term investments.
- Is not leveraged except for a minimal amount on a short-term basis.
- Does not offer redemption rights to its investors.
- Represents itself to investors as pursuing a venture capital strategy.

Private Fund Advisers With Less Than $150 Million in Assets Under Management in the U.S. An exemption for private fund advisers with less than $150 million in assets under management in the United States.

Foreign Private Advisers. The Dodd-Frank Act also amended the Advisers Act to provide for an exemption from registration for foreign advisers that do not have a place of business in the United States, and have:

- Less than $25 million in aggregate assets under management from U.S. clients and private fund investors.
- Fewer than 15 U.S. clients and private fund investors.

Investment Company Act of 1940: When used in this title, "investment company" means any issuer which (A) is or holds itself out as being engaged primarily, or proposes to engage primarily, in the business of investing, reinvesting, or trading in securities; (B) is engaged or proposes to engage in the business of issuing face-amount certificates of the installment type, or has been engaged in such business and has any such certificate outstanding; or (C) is engaged or proposes to engage in the business of investing, reinvesting, holding, or trading in securities, and owns or proposes to acquire investment securities having a value exceeding 40 percent of the value of such issuer's total assets (exclusive of Government securities and cash items) on an unconsolidated basis. So the following <u>exemptions</u> may apply to your hedge fund:

Section 3(c)(1) Exemption - A 3(c)(1) hedge fund is exempt under the Investment Company Act provided that the fund is beneficially owned by not more than 100 investors and is not making a public offering of its securities.

Section 3(c)(7) Exemption – A 3(c)(7) hedge fund is exempt under the Investment Company Act and must comply with two basic requirements: (1) the fund can have only qualified purchasers as investors and (2) the fund can have no more than 499 investors.

All of the above Federal regulations and exemptions pertain to a U.S. based investment manager managing a U.S. based hedge fund containing U.S. investors (individuals, corporations, partnerships, trusts, etc.). If you decide on trading Forex, Commodities, Futures, and Options on Futures, then there is a possibility that you will need to adhere to some further regulations (with possible exemptions).

The Investment Advisers Act Investor Criteria.

Under the Investment Advisers Act of 1940 (the Advisers Act), it identifies who can invest in your fund, depending upon the fee structure of the offering. Where there is a performance fee, a special allocation fee, or a general fee tied to the performance of the fund, the Advisers Act requires that sales be made only to a "qualified client" or investor. As defined in Rule 205-3 of the SEC, a "qualified client" is:

- A natural person who or a company that immediately after entering into the contract has at least $1,000,000 under the management of the investment adviser; or
- A natural person who or a company that the investment adviser entering into the contract (and any person acting on his behalf) reasonably believes, immediately prior to entering into the contract, either:
  - Has a net worth (together, in the case of a natural person, with assets held jointly with a spouse) of more than $2 million at the time the contract is entered into; or

- A natural person who immediately prior to entering into the contract is:
    o An executive officer, director, trustee, general partner or person serving in a similar capacity, of the investment adviser; or
    o An employee of the investment adviser (other than an employee performing solely clerical, secretarial, or administrative functions with regard to the investment adviser) who, in connection with his or her regular functions or duties, participates in the investment activities of such investment adviser, provided that such employee has been performing such functions and duties for or on behalf of the investment adviser, or substantially similar functions or duties for or on behalf of another company for at least 12 months.

You can see that the net asset threshold of your accredited investor has increased from $1,000,000 (as stated in Regulation D) to $2,000,000 (as stated in the Advisers Act). Keep in mind that this only applies IF you intend on earning a performance fee from your investors, which is the case when operating your hedge fund.

Trading Futures, Commodities, and Forex

Some fund managers choose to trade futures and/or commodities and/or FOREX (foreign exchange) in their trading portfolio. Generally, such managers will need to register as commodity pool operators ("CPO") and as commodity trading advisors ("CTA") if their hedge fund will be domiciled in the U.S. The hedge fund itself will be deemed to be a commodity pool. For purposes of the Commodities Exchange Act ("CEA"), a future and commodity are functionally equal as it relates to hedge fund manager registration.

According to the National Futures Association (NFA) to qualify for registration as a Commodity Trading Advisor, a CTA is an individual or organization (domiciled in the U.S.) which, for compensation or profit, advises others as to the value of or the advisability of buying or selling futures contracts, options on futures, retail off-exchange Forex contracts or swaps.

Providing advice includes exercising trading authority over a customer's account as well as giving advice based upon knowledge of or tailored to customer's particular commodity interest account, particular commodity interest trading activity, or other similar types of information.

Registration is required <u>unless</u>:

- You have provided advice to 15 or fewer persons during the past 12 months and do not generally hold yourself out to the public as a CTA or
- You are in one of a number of businesses or professions listed in the Commodity Exchange Act or are registered in another capacity and your advice is solely incidental to your principal business or profession or
- You are providing advice that is not based upon knowledge of or tailored to customer's particular commodity interest account, particular commodity interest trading activity, or other similar types of information, such as, for example
- You make recommendations, such as advice to buy or sell specific futures contracts should a particular price level be reached, through newsletters, books, and periodicals. The advice includes specific recommendations and the recipients of publications all receive the same advice or
- You provide specific advice through e-mails, facsimiles, an Internet web site, telephone calls or face-to-face meetings with customers consisting of instructions to buy or sell a futures contract based on a computerized trading system, which also is available for purchase and use on a personal computer, and the customers all receive the same advice or
- You conduct seminars at which you teach attendees how to trade commodity futures contracts aided by a software program that you sell and you invite seminar attendees to participate in a question-and-answer session at which you provide commodity trading advice without asking or receiving information about the personal characteristics of the attendees.

9

U.S. Commodity Futures Trading Commission: In addition, the U.S. Commodity Futures Trading Commission (CFTC) has provided certain exemptions from registering as a CTA. According to the CFTC, the following exemptions can be relied upon:

Exemption from Registration as a CTA. Section 4m(1) of the Commodity Exchange Act provides an exemption from registration for a person who, in the preceding twelve months, has not furnished commodity trading advice to more than 15 persons and who does not hold himself out generally to the public as a CTA.

Section 4m(3) provides an exemption from CTA registration for a person: (1) who is registered with the Securities and Exchange Commission as an investment adviser; (2) whose business does not consist primarily of acting as a commodity trading advisor; and (3) who does not act as a commodity trading advisor to any investment trust, syndicate, or similar form of enterprise that is engaged primarily in trading in any commodity for future delivery on or subject to the rules of any contract market or registered derivatives transaction execution facility.

Exemption From Registration as a CPO. Rule 4.13 (17 C.F.R. § 4.13) makes available an exemption from commodity pool operator registration for certain persons. Broadly speaking, these persons are the operators of "family, club and small" pools, as those terms are defined in the rule, as well as pools that have limited futures activity or that restrict participation to sophisticated persons.

Exemption from Certain Part 4 Requirements Where Participants are "Qualified Eligible Persons". Rule 4.7 (17 C.F.R. 4.7) makes available an exemption from certain Part 4 requirements with respect to the operators of commodity pools whose participants are limited to "qualified eligible persons" and with respect to commodity trading advisors who advise "qualified eligible persons," as defined in the Rule. Briefly stated, "QEPs" include such persons as certain investment professionals, knowledgeable employees, qualified purchasers, non-United States persons, and accredited investors who meet a portfolio requirement.

Exemption from Certain Part 4 Requirements Where Pool Meets Certain Trading Criteria. Rule 4.12(b) (17 C.F.R. 4.12) provides an exemption from certain Part 4 requirements for the operators of certain commodity pools. Among other things, the pools these CPOs operate do not commit more than 10% of the fair market value of their assets to establish commodity interest trading positions and they trade commodity interests in a manner solely incidental to their securities trading activities.

These are just the main exemptions that a U.S. based fund manager/hedge fund should rely on. You hedge fund consultant along with your securities attorney will properly advise you on the proper formation and legal regulatory requirements.

The European Union Alternative Investment Fund Managers Directive (AIFMD): For those who intend on marketing their funds to investors located in the European Union (EU), there is another set of rules which need to be adhered to. This pertains to the U.S. or non-EU managers/funds who market to EU investors.

In July 2013, the EU created the framework for AIFMD for alternative investment funds as well as to increase protection for investors. The directive also aims to lessen the exposure to risks through a uniform framework for regulating alternative investment funds or AIFs across the EU region. The AIFMD allows fund managers within the EU to sell alternative investment funds (AIFs) to professional investors through the use of a passporting system, in which fund managers are subjected to the regulations of their home countries. I will focus on non-EU managers/funds and how this directive will affect the marketing of the fund.

Fund managers who are managing anywhere other than the EU, such as the United States, but are marketing their hedge funds in the EU are subject to certain parts of the directive. Marketing under the directive pertains to the "at the initiative of the manager or on behalf of the manager" among EU investors. This means that those who are engaged in passive marketing, or manage a fund of which the investor initiated the purchase, are not covered by the AIFMD. But a fund manager from the US who uses a placement or distribution agent will be subjected to the directive. These fund managers need to make sure that the EU member states in which they are selling have some sort of private placement regulations (and exemptions) in place and that they may register with the regulators of each of those EU member countries. The AIFMD will NOT apply to:

- AIFMs managing AIFs that have total assets of less than

€100 million; or

- AIFMs managing AIFs that have total assets of less than €500 million subject to the AIFs not being leveraged and have no redemption rights during a period of 5 years following the date of the initial investment in each AIF.

AIFMs located outside the EU who can accept subscriptions from EU investors ONLY if they do not initiate the approach (reverse solicitation/inquiry).

Marketing or Soft Marketing. Marketing is defined in the Directive as involving an "offer" of units or shares in a fund to prospective investors. "Soft" marketing to investors with early-stage documents cannot technically be an "offer" since there is nothing that can yet be legally accepted. Use general material such as pitch book, slide presentation, etc. should be acceptable provided that you restrict the number of people who receive this material and take back copies that are not absolutely necessary.

This is just an overview of some of the main regulations any start-up fund manager will need to grasp. Don't worry about trying to remember it all. This is the job of your securities attorney.

2
SELECTING YOUR INVESTMENT STYLE & STRATEGY

By way of definition, the term "Alternative Investments" can be defined as investment securities trading outside traditional investments like stocks, bonds, cash or real estate. The alternative investment industry includes hedge funds, funds of hedge funds, managed futures funds and other non-traditional asset classes.

Investment managers are renowned by their purpose to deliver absolute returns, despite market conditions. Using strategy-driven and research-backed investment methods, alternative managers try to provide a wide asset base as well as benefits such as lowered volatility (risk) and the probability of improved performance.

Hedge Funds

A hedge fund is a name used to describe an investment partnership created by an investment manager. The hedge fund can be a limited partnership or a limited liability company. These two entity structures are the legal choices in the U.S. so that if the company/fund goes bankrupt, the creditors can't go after the investors for more money than they've put into the hedge fund.

Funds of Funds

Fund of Funds is simply hedge funds that invest in other hedge funds. Typically, the fund manager will diversify the fund's assets by allocating capital to other various fund styles or strategies. Funds of hedge funds merely follow this strategy by constructing a portfolio of other hedge funds. How the underlying hedge funds are selected can differ. A fund of hedge funds may invest only in hedge funds using a particular management strategy. Or, a fund of hedge funds may invest in hedge funds using many different strategies in an effort to gain exposure to all of them.

Investment Styles and Strategies

Some countries have set up a classification structure for the hedge funds that register for business in their markets, while others have not. Because of this, there is no global standard for classifying funds into different investment style peer groups. Below is the group structure that Bloomberg utilizes.

Funds are first broken down into distinct Investment Strategies, which is further refined into the separate Investment Styles.

Emerging Market

This strategy involves investments in equity or fixed income securities of companies, or sovereigns, located in "emerging" countries and markets. These areas include parts of Asia and the former Soviet Union, Eastern Europe, Latin America, and Africa. Managers typically hold mostly long positions due to the lack of derivatives and futures markets, and also because emerging markets often do not allow short sales.

Styles **Emerging Market Debt** - An Emerging Market investment style that invests primarily in fixed income securities in emerging markets. These areas include parts of Asia and the former Soviet Union, Eastern Europe, Latin America, and Africa.

Style **Emerging Market Equity** - An Emerging Market investment style that invests primarily in equity securities, in emerging markets. These areas include parts of Asia and the former Soviet Union, Eastern Europe, Latin America, and Africa.

Equity Directional

This strategy involves directional investments in equity markets. This means managers will take a 'top-down' approach to develop a portfolio. Managers will look at market movements, news, and trends, and also look to news and movements of specific sectors or market caps, in an attempt to gauge where opportunities will arise.

The securities selected to make up the Portfolio will come from the broad research of the markets and sectors, narrowed down to the securities which match the investment needs. Portfolios can shift from value to growth stocks; from sector to sector; or even vary in market capitalization focus. Investment styles include Long/Short Equity, Long Biased Equity and Short Biased Equity.

Styles **Long/Short Equity** - An Equity Directional investment style employs both long and short equity positions. The Fund's goal is not to be market neutral, but rather to switch back and forth between an overall net long or net short portfolio, depending on market conditions and opportunities where a Manager sees differences between a securities value and market price. Investments will usually be regional or sector-specific.

Style **Long Biased Equity** - An Equity Directional investment style employing both long and short equity positions. Funds will invest primarily in long positions in securities expected to appreciate in value while supplementing that with short positions of securities expected to fall in value. Investments will usually be regional or sector-specific. This also includes funds which invest in private placements, or 'Regulation D' securities, which are privately offered securities offered to the fund, upon negotiated terms since they are highly illiquid.

Style **Short Biased Equity** - An Equity Directional investment style that employs short, and sometimes long, equity positions. Funds will invest in short positions in securities expected to fall in value and maybe supplementing that with long positions of securities expected to appreciate in value. Investments will usually be regional or sector-specific.

Equity Market Neutral

This strategy involves investing in a non-directional equity portfolio. This means managers will have a selection of securities they are interested in trading but will research the company's fundamentals and past performance, before expanding to a broader sector-wide or market-wide analysis. Funds will balance long and short exposures in the market, usually resulting in a beta and/or currency-neutral portfolio. The long and short positions are intended to take advantage of specific market movements and not be affected by overall market direction. An example is where a fund will be short a portfolio of companies which are not showing signs of growth while being long a portfolio of companies which are. Investment styles include Equity Fundamental Market Neutral and Equity Statistical Arbitrage.

Style **Equity Fundamental Market Neutral** – An Equity Market Neutral investment style that attempts to take advantage of pricing inefficiencies in the equity markets. Funds will utilize a fundamental "bottom-up" investment style when selecting the long and short positions in their portfolios.

Style **Equity Statistical Arbitrage** – An Equity Market Neutral investment style that attempts to take advantage of pricing discrepancies in the equity markets. Funds will utilize mathematical models or calculations to evaluate a portfolio of stocks, and attempt to profit from variations of current prices compared to similar stocks and/or historical performance norms. One common technique is known as 'Pairs Trading'.

Event-Driven

This strategy attempts to take advantage of pricing fluctuations of securities due to corporate events or actions. These situations include corporate restructuring, mergers, takeovers, liquidations, bankruptcy, spinoffs and re-organizations. Investment styles include Distressed Securities and Merger Arbitrage.

Style **Distressed Securities** – An Event-Driven investment style that attempts to invest in companies whose stock price is being unfairly punished due to financial, legal or operating difficulties, like reorganization, restructuring, bankruptcy. The manager feels a securities price will change rapidly due to a stock buyback, bond upgrade, spin-off or earnings surprise. Investments may be made through equity, debt or other securities. Funds focused on distressed debt may also use the terms 'high-yield' or 'junk bonds' to refer to the non-investment grade debt securities they invest in. Although distressed debt is usually considered a step below high-yield, for the purposes of classification we will place high yield funds into the Distressed Securities peer group.

Style **Merger Arbitrage** – An Event-Driven investment style that attempts to exploit pricing inefficiencies in Merger & Acquisition events. Merger Arbitrage funds seek to capture the price spread between the current market price of a security and its value after a successfully completed merger transaction. Funds usually invest short in the acquiring company and invest long in the acquired company, continually modifying their positions as the merger process moves forward. This is because when mergers or acquisitions are announced, there is a general trend for the acquiring company's stock value to drop and the acquired company's stock value to rise.

Fixed Income Directional

This strategy invests in debt securities without utilizing arbitrage or hedging techniques. Funds will usually hold long positions in debt instruments believed to be undervalued or to profit from movements in interest rates. Investment styles include High Yield, Asset-Backed Securities and Fixed Income.

Style **Asset-Backed Securities** – A Fixed Income Directional investment style in which funds will invest in securities backed by notes or receivables against assets other than real estate. Some examples are autos, credit cards, and royalties.

Style **Fixed Income** – A Fixed Income Directional investment style in which funds typically hold long positions, but may also invest on the short side, in debt securities. This includes government, corporate and other types of debt instruments, fixed income options and credit derivatives. Funds will attempt to profit from credit and yield opportunities in fixed income markets.

Fixed Income Relative Value

This strategy involves investments in debt securities, with an emphasis on either exploiting inefficiencies or capturing yield spreads between market segments. Funds will invest in fixed income securities or sectors and hedge their exposure to interest rate movements, currency exposure, and other risks. This includes investments in government bonds, convertibles, corporate bonds, interest rate swaps, and mortgage-backed securities. Investment styles include Fixed Income Arbitrage, Convertible Arbitrage, Mortgage-Backed Arbitrage, and Capital Structure Arbitrage.

Style **Fixed Income Arbitrage** – A Fixed Income Relative Value investment style that attempts to take advantage of risk spreads and pricing inefficiencies of sovereign, corporate and other types of debt securities. Funds will usually employ techniques such as yield-curve or spread arbitrage using municipal and corporate debt securities hedged with Treasury bonds or other financial contracts. This includes credit arbitrage techniques as well.

Style **Convertible Arbitrage** – A Fixed Income Relative Value investment style that looks to exploit inefficiencies in pricing between convertible debt securities and the common stocks of the same company. Funds will usually buy convertible bonds or preferred stock and short the underlying common stock, creating a portfolio that can profit from extreme moves, up or down, in the stock. Funds may also attempt to hedge against interest rate exposure.

Style **Capital Structure Arbitrage** - A Fixed Income Relative Value investment style that is similar to Convertible Arbitrage, however, Capital Structure Arbitrage attempts to exploit the mispricing of different classes of securities of the same company. If a company has more than one class of debt or stock, each class represents the value of their contingent claim on the company. Different valuations and trading inefficiencies can lead to arbitrage opportunities between classes, with a properly constructed portfolio.

Style **Mortgage-Backed Arbitrage** – A Fixed Income Relative Value investment style that attempts to capture the spread inherent in Mortgage-Backed Securities by using interest rate futures, options, and treasury securities. This investment requires a careful analysis of the changes in mortgage-backed securities due to interest rate fluctuations to maintain a properly hedged portfolio. A typical investment would be long Mortgage-Backed Security and short government bonds and other financial instruments or contracts.

Managed Futures/CTA

This strategy attempts to profit by investing in listed financial and commodity futures markets and currency markets. Managed Futures funds invest in futures and options contacts of equity and debt securities, commodities, and currencies.

Style **CTA/Managed Futures** – A Managed Futures investment style that attempts to take advantage of market inefficiencies by investing in any and all types of futures and options contracts for equity and fixed income securities, currencies or commodities. Some Funds are registered Commodities Trading Advisors and are referred to as CTA's.

Global Macro

This strategy invests using a "top-down" approach. Funds will use leveraging techniques on perceived price-value disparities of stock markets, interest rates, foreign exchange rates, and commodities. Manager's strategies are usually based around an opportunistic approach to global economies and their policies, although funds may focus their investments in specific countries or regions.

Styles **Macro** – This Global Macro investment style invests using a "top-down" approach. Funds will use leveraging techniques on perceived price-value disparities of stock markets, interest rates, foreign exchange rates, and commodities. Manager's strategies are usually based around an opportunistic approach to global economies and their policies, although funds may focus their investments in specific countries or regions. Some Managers will use systematic (mathematical) models to find and execute all trades while others will use fundamental analysis and human input to decide where and when to invest.

Multi-Strategy/Multi-Style

Funds which utilize multiple investment strategies and/or multiple investment styles will be categorized as such. Some funds employ several strategies within their own portfolio, while others will invest their assets in other hedge funds that run the desired investment strategy/style (Fund of Funds).

If there are funds whose investment strategies/styles are so unique that they do not fit into an existing peer group, or if there are not enough funds with the same strategy/style to warrant their own peer group, then they will be categorized under Multi-Strategy/Multi-Style.

Whatever your strategy or style is, it's important to note that you will need to properly describe this in your offering memorandum. Your hedge fund consultant and your attorney will tweak any wording so that it will not appear to be misleading or false. Also, you may consider having a multi-asset fund involving a variety of securities such as futures, options, precious metals, and Forex.

3
HOW MUCH ARE YOU WORTH?

Given that hedge funds are unregistered investment companies, its fee structure is unregulated as well, therefore giving you a vast amount of freedom to charge fees to your fund.

In the U.S. a hedge fund is either structured as a limited liability company or a limited partnership. Most hedge funds utilize the limited partnership structure but from my personal experience I have set up both. Typically it's a matter of preference.

Management Fees

Roughly all hedge funds charge a management fee. The fee is typically between one and two percent of the asset under management per year. I have set up funds that charge up to three percent (though that is not common). The management fee is typically assessed monthly to help cover the cost of running a hedge fund.

Pursuant to the Limited Partnership Agreement, let's assume your fund will pay you, the General Partner (that is you, the investment manager) a management fee, monthly in advance, equal to 0.146% (or 1.75% per annum) with respect to Class A Limited Partners and 0.125% (or 1.50% per annum) with respect to Class B Limited Partners of the net asset value of the capital accounts of the Limited Partners (This example is for hedge funds who choose to have multi-class units with specific minimum investment, performance fee, lock period, etc.). The management fee would be assessed pro-rata to each Limited Partner. If a new or existing Partner makes a contribution to your fund on any day other than the beginning of the month, the General Partner shall be entitled to a pro-rated management fee at that time. Management fees are typically nonrefundable. However, you, the General Partner does have the right to waive all or a part of the management fee with respect to one or more Limited Partners from time to time in your sole discretion. The General Partner may also pay over a portion of the management fee to one or more third parties who introduce investors or perform other services for your hedge fund or the General Partner.

Performance Fees

This is also known as an incentive fee or carried interest. Like the management fee, almost all hedge funds assess a performance fee as a component of their fee structure. Typically, this fee is 20 percent of returns. The profits and losses of the fund will be provisionally allocated among the capital accounts of the Partners and the General Partner (collectively, the "Partners") at the end of each calendar period in proportion to the relative values of such capital accounts at the beginning of such calendar period.

Then, at the close of each Performance Period but subject to the "high water mark" limitation discussed below, the applicable percentage in a two-class hedge fund (20% for Class A Limited Partners and 16% for Class B Limited Partners) of the net profits (realized and unrealized) in excess of the "Hurdle Rate."

High Water Mark. The performance fee allocable to you as the General Partner is subject to a "high water mark" limitation so that no allocation is made to the General Partner with respect to its performance fee until prior net losses allocated to a Limited Partner are recouped. The amount of prior period net losses that must be recouped before a performance fee allocation is made shall be adjusted to take into account any distributions to or withdrawals by a Partner, with the amount of such prior net losses being reduced in proportion to the distribution or withdrawal. This protects investors from paying excessive and redundant performance fees. A high-water mark limits or eliminates the performance fee for making back a loss.

Hurdle Rate. Hurdle rates also referred to as minimum acceptable rates of return, are also used as a factor for hedge fund performance fees, by measuring fund performance against a particular benchmark such as LIBOR. Though not required, in the event you do utilize hurdle rate, then performance fee percentages are not paid to the fund manager/General Partner unless the rate of return on the fund meets or exceeds that benchmark rate.

Once the profits have exceeded the high water mark (and hurdle rate if applied), then the performance fee or carried interest is provisionally allocated to the capital account of each Limited Partner or, in the case of a withdrawal of capital by a Partner other than on the last day of the year, to the withdrawing Partner with respect to the withdrawn Interest as if the withdrawal date was the last day of the year, shall be reallocated and credited to the capital account of the General Partner and debited to the capital accounts of the Limited Partners or the withdrawing Limited Partner, as the case may be.

The reallocation of net profits to the General Partner described above represents the General Partner's performance fee or "Carried Interest" in the fund. The "Performance Period" is the calendar year; provided, however, that (a) if a Partner is admitted to the fund on any date other than the first day of the year, then the initial Performance Period shall be the period commencing on such date and ending on the last day of the year, (b) upon the withdrawal of capital by a Partner other than at the end of the year, the Performance Period shall be the period commencing on the first day of the year or on the date during the year in which the capital account was established, if other than the first day of the year, and ending on the withdrawal date, and (c) in the event the fund is terminated other than at the end of a year, the final Performance Period shall be the period commencing on the first day of the fund's final calendar year and ending on the termination date. The General Partner's Carried Interest is not affected by net losses in a subsequent calendar period.

Profits and losses will be accrued on a monthly basis but generally will be allocated to the capital accounts of the Partners only at the end of each calendar year and upon the withdrawal or expulsion of a Partner if such withdrawal or expulsion occurs on a day other than the end of a calendar year.

The profits or losses of the fund for a particular period will be measured in terms of the increase or decrease in the net assets of the fund from the beginning to the end of the period, after giving effect to the expenses of the Fund for such period. In calculating profits or losses, securities are typically valued on a "marked-to-market" basis provided that you are trading traditional securities such as listed stocks, bonds, options, commodities, etc., with the result that the profits or losses for a particular period will not necessarily reflect amounts which have been or will be realized or sustained. In other words, you earn the performance fee on unrealized gains without having to sell the securities and earn a profit.

As the General Partner, you may waive all or part of the performance fee or carried interest with respect to one or more Partners from time to time in your sole discretion. The General Partner may also pay over or cause your fund to reallocate a portion of the Performance Allocation to one or more third parties who introduce investors or perform other services for the Fund or the General Partner.

So, the question to ask is; "how much am I worth to handle and manage this fund"? There is no easy or straight answer. I do advise my clients to take into consideration that new funds need to attract new investors. Investors are not only shopping around other funds with similar strategies and styles but looking at the lowest fees. The industry norm is 2/20. 2% annual management and 20% performance fee or carried interest. You can always offer a discounted arrangement to new investors in exchange for the seed capital. Then at some point after you have a certain amount of assets under management (AUM) you can raise the rates to its initial levels.

Other Fees and Expenses

Your hedge fund shall pay, or reimburse the you, General Partner/Investment Manager, all reasonable costs and expenses (including the fees and expenses of counsel and accountants) incurred by or on behalf of your hedge fund in connection with the formation and operation of your fund and the offering and sale of the Interests, including: all costs, fees and expenses of your hedge fund directly related to the purchase, sale or retention of securities or other property by your fund (including all fees and commissions of brokers and custodians, all fees and disbursements of outside attorneys and accountants, all fees and expenses relating to the registration and qualification for sale of such securities and all transfer taxes); all U.S. federal, state and local taxes and filing fees payable by your fund; all costs, fees and expenses of your fund relating to Partners' meetings and the preparation and mailing of reports to Limited Partners; all fees and disbursements of your fund's outside attorneys, accountants and consultants; all filing and recording fees; (vi) all interest expense of your fund; and any extraordinary expenses of your fund; and all expenses in connection with marketing of your hedge fund. As a general rule, your hedge fund will not be liable for any of the general overhead expenses of the General Partner (such as rent, salaries, and equipment costs). All such overhead expenses are for the account of the General Partner. Also, the organization costs of your hedge fund are tabulated based on your invoices and credited back to you as well as amortize typically over a period of up to 60 months.

4
PUTTING IT ALL TOGETHER: SETTING THE RULES FOR MANAGING YOUR FUND

One of the challenges that most new fund managers face is setting the rules which govern admitting new investors, redemptions, and operations.

Capital Contributions

Unless otherwise determined by you, at your discretion, each new Partner/investor (assuming you will be using a Limited Partnership structure) shall be admitted to your fund, and each existing Partner may make an additional capital contribution to your fund, as of the first day of a calendar month provided that you timely receives and accepts such person's initial or additional, as applicable, capital contribution and executed Subscription Documents or such other documents or agreements as you or Administrator may require. A person shall become a Limited Partner when you enter such person as a Limited Partner on the books of your fund. Capital contributions must be made in cash unless you, in your sole discretion, agree to accept capital contributions in-kind.

Your Limited Partners typically may make withdrawals of capital on 30 days' prior written notice to you as the General Partner/Investment Manager at the end of the relevant Lock-Up Period (one-year lock-up is standard) and at the end of each calendar quarter thereafter. You can choose to redeem monthly however, keep in mind that your strategy can be negatively affected by selling or disrupting your portfolio if you opt to choose this. You also have absolute discretion to deny or permit a partial withdrawal of your Partner's capital if, after giving effect to such withdrawal, the value of the Partner's capital account would be less than the initial investment, and you may treat any such request for partial withdrawal as a request for withdrawal of the Partner's entire Interest. Distribution of any withdrawal generally should be made within 15 days after the withdrawal date, although 10% of any withdrawal that represents more than 90% of a Partner's capital may be withheld until your fund receives its audited financial statements for the calendar year during which the withdrawal was made. You may vary these withdrawal terms, in whole or part, for certain investors, at your sole discretion.

The right of any Limited Partner or its legal representatives to withdraw any amount from its capital account and to have distributed to it any such amount (or any portion thereof) is subject to the provision set by you for all fund's liabilities in accordance with applicable Delaware law (I recommend Delaware for U.S. based funds) and for reserves for contingencies and estimated accrued expenses and liabilities. In addition, no withdrawal should be permitted that would result in a Partner's capital account having a negative balance. The unused portion of any reserve will be distributed to the Partners to which the reserve applies after you shall have determined that the need, therefore, shall have ceased.

You, as the General Partner may provide written notice to your Partners to suspend withdrawal rights, in whole or in part, when there exists a state of affairs in which disposal of your fund's assets and liabilities, or the determination of the value of the withdrawing Partners' capital accounts, would not be reasonably practicable or would be prejudicial to the non-withdrawing Partners. In addition, you as the General Partner/Investment Manager may suspend payment of withdrawal proceeds payable to such Partner if you reasonably deem it necessary to do so to comply with anti-money laundering laws and regulations applicable to your fund, you or any of your fund's service providers.

"*Lock-Up Period*" means with respect to having a fund with two class of shares, with respect to Class A Limited Partners, the period of six months after the date of a Limited Partner's capital contribution during which such Limited Partner may not withdraw any part of such Limited Partner's capital account related to such capital contribution unless such Limited Partner pays a withdrawal fee equal to let's say, 3% of the amount withdrawn and with respect to Class B Limited Partners, the period of two years after the date of a Limited Partner's capital contribution during which such Limited Partner may not withdraw any part of such Limited Partner's capital account related to such capital contribution. Keep in mind that this is only an example. You may also opt to issue one class of shares which is standard.

The Lock-Up Period normally is calculated separately for each capital contribution made by your Limited Partner. For these purposes, withdrawals of capital will be processed on a "first-in, first-out" basis, with each withdrawal being made with reference to the earliest available capital contribution.

Compliance

New fund managers often overlook this important task because they are so focused on attracting investors. It's just as important to conduct basic Know Your Client (KYC) procedures as it is to qualify an investment fund. Even as a hedge fund consultant, I have to pre-qualify every new prospective client before I even engage in any conversation with them. It's not a complicated process.

When you get an indication of interest from a prospective investor, the first thing you should consider doing is a quick Google search of their name, company and anything that relates to their inquiries. I also subscribe to a background check service called Beenverified.com. For about $100 per year, you can look up someone based on the first, last name and state they live. You can see if they have any criminal or civil records (BK, Liens, etc). Another compliance tool is Lexis Nexis. For global clients you can try WorldCheck. All these background check tools come with a price. But it's worth it.

However, in order for your investors/partners to invest in your fund, they will have to provide you with basic due diligence documentation. As part of your fund's responsibility for the prevention of money laundering, your fund, the General Partner and your administrator will require a detailed verification of an investor's identity and the source of the payment from any person delivering completed Subscription Documents to your fund.

In order to comply with proposed regulations aimed at the

prevention of money laundering in the United States, your fund is required to verify the identity of all prospective investors and the source of their funds, to the extent required under the USA PATRIOT Act, and to determine if such investors are Prohibited Investors (as defined in your fund's Subscription Documents) identified on various lists maintained by the U.S. Government. If your fund determines that any investor is a Prohibited Investor, your fund may, among other things, freeze that investor's assets in your fund and notify appropriate legal authorities.

Your fund, the General Partner, and your administrator reserve the right to request such documentation as they deem necessary to verify the identity of a prospective investor and to verify the source of the relevant subscription amounts. The amount of detail required will depend on the circumstances of each application for subscription. By way of example, an individual subscriber may be required to produce a copy of a passport or driver's license, together with evidence of his/her address, such as a utility bill or bank statement, and date of birth. For corporate subscribers, your fund may require the production of copies of their certificates of incorporation or other formation documents (and any changes of name) and information concerning their principals or beneficial owners. Advise your potential investor that failure to provide the necessary evidence may result in his subscription application being rejected or delayed in the processing of withdrawals.

If, within a reasonable period of time following a request for verification of identity, you have not received satisfactory evidence of a subscriber's identity, then you may, in your absolute discretion, reject the subscription, in which subscription money will be returned without interest to the account from which such sums of money were originally debited. You and any agent of your fund and the General Partner will be held harmless and will be fully indemnified by a potential subscriber against any loss arising as a result of a failure to process a subscription or withdrawal request if such information as has been requested by any of them has not been satisfactorily provided by the applicant.

If you have a suspicion that a payment to your fund (by way of subscription or otherwise) or a payment from your fund (by way of withdrawal or otherwise) contains the proceeds of criminal conduct, you may report such suspicion to the appropriate authorities. Neither you, your fund nor the General Partner will incur any liability for adhering to your fund's responsibilities under its anti-money laundering program, and they will be indemnified by the Subscriber for any losses which they or their respective principals, employees or agents may incur for doing so.

Your investors need to be qualified as well. Your fund offering is made available to what is described as eligible "purchasers" (for a U.S. fund each purchaser of an Interest is being referred to as a "Limited Partner"). Investment in your fund might not be suitable for certain other tax-exempt investors. Only investors who are: (i) "accredited investors" in the meaning of Rule 501 of Regulation D under the Securities Act; (ii) "qualified clients," as defined in Rule 205-3 under the Advisers Act; and (iii) knowledgeable and experienced in management and business matters such that they are capable of evaluating the merits and risks of an investment in your fund will be permitted to invest in your fund.

An "accredited investor" includes (i) natural persons who have a net worth, taken together with the net worth of their spouse, in excess of $1 million (excluding personal residence) or who had individual income of more than $200,000 in each of the prior two calendar years, or joint income with their spouse in excess of $300,000 for each of those years, and who reasonably expect to reach the same income level in the current year; (ii) investment partnerships and other entities all of whose equity owners are accredited investors; and (iii) entities with assets in excess of $5 million. A "qualified client" includes persons having at least $1,000,000 invested in your fund or otherwise with the General Partner, or persons having a net worth (together, in the case of a natural person, with assets held jointly with a spouse and exclusive of personal residence) of more than $2,000,000 at the time of their subscription.

Here is a text taken from a hedge fund subscription agreement's Anti-Money Laundering Certification Form in which your investors would have to complete and sign off on:

Anti-Money Laundering Certification Form
(SAMPLE)

The undersigned, being the_____ of_____ a_____ organized under the laws of_____,(the "Subscriber Entity"), does hereby certify on behalf of the Subscriber Entity that it is aware of the requirements of the USA PATRIOT Act of

2001, the regulations administered by the U.S. Department of the Treasury's Office of Foreign Assets Control and the anti-money laundering laws and regulations as established in its jurisdiction of organization (collectively, the "anti-money laundering/OFAC laws"). The Subscriber Entity has anti-money laundering policies and procedures in place reasonably designed to verify the identity of the beneficial owners of the investment in the Fund and their sources of funds. Such policies and procedures are properly enforced and are consistent with the anti-money laundering/OFAC laws such that the Fund may rely on this Certification.

The Subscriber Entity hereby represents to the Fund that, to the best of its knowledge, the beneficial owners of the investment in the Fund are not individuals, entities or countries that may subject the Fund to criminal or civil violations of anti-money laundering/OFAC laws. The Subscriber Entity has read the Subscriber's Subscription Agreement. The Subscriber Entity has taken all reasonable steps to ensure that the owners of the investment in the Fund are able to make to such representations. The Subscriber Entity agrees promptly to notify the Fund should the Subscriber Entity have any questions relating to any of the investors or become aware of any changes in the representations set forth in this Certification.

Date:

By:
Name:

List of Investor KYC Documents

The following are a list of documents your investors are required to submit to you and your administrator prior to being accepted in to your fund.

For Individual Investors:
- Completed Subscription Documents duly executed.
- Copy of passport or other government-issued picture identification duly certified.
- Separate proof of current address (e.g. a utility bill dated within the last two months).
- Bank or Professional reference (case-by-case)

For Corporations & Other Entities
- Completed Subscription Documents duly signed by authorized signatories.
- Copies of formation documents (e.g. certificate of incorporation, by-laws, trust deed, partnership agreement, etc. and, upon request, evidence of current good standing to conduct business.)
- A copy of current offering memorandum if the Subscriber is a fund-of-funds.
- Copy of authorized signatories list.

From Subscriber to Investor

To become an Investor, your Subscriber should:

- complete and execute a copy of the Subscription Documents, inserting the amount of the capital contribution agreed to be made. He should also include his personal information and taxpayer identification or social security number;
- provide copies of documents confirming the investor's identification, such as a passport or driver's license;
- deliver all such documents to your administrator.

All capital contributions should be made by wiring cash to your fund's bank account in the name of your fund which is typically received at least three business days prior to the subscription date.

You, as the General Partner may pay fees to persons (whether or not affiliated with the General Partner) who are instrumental in the sale of Interests in your fund.

In making the investment decision to invest in your fund, your prospective Investor must rely on their own examination of your fund and the terms of the offering outline in your Offering Memorandum and Subscription Agreement, including the merits and significant risks involved. You should advise each prospective Investor to consult his own counsel, accountants, and other professional advisers as to investment, legal, tax and other related matters concerning such proposed investment.

5
UNDERSTANDING YOUR OFFERING DOCUMENTS

Your hedge fund offering documents consist of the following set of documents:

- Private Placement Memorandum
- Subscription Agreement
- Limited Partnership Agreement

PRIVATE PLACEMENT MEMORANDUM

The crux of your hedge fund offering is your Private Placement Memorandum (PPM). Also called Private Offering Memorandum and Confidential Information Memorandum. Within your PPM contains the following important topics:

- Summary
- Directory
- Introduction
- Investment Activities of the Fund
- Management Company of the Fund
- Administrator
- Auditor
- Valuation of Fund's Assets

- Anti-Money Laundering Considerations
- Certain Federal Income Tax Considerations
- Securities Laws
- Reports to Partners (Investors)
- Subscriptions Procedures
- Risk Factors

This is the way I typically prepare offering documents for my clients which are always reviewed and modified by one of my qualified securities attorneys depending on each situation and jurisdiction.

The Summary

Your Summary will contain the following general information:

Name of your Fund: Includes the name of your fund, where is it registered (ex. Delaware limited partnership formed on x date). It also states that the fund is being operated pursuant to an exemption from registration with the U.S. Securities and Exchange Commission (the "SEC") as an investment company under Section 3(c)(1) of the U.S. Investment Company Act of 1940, as amended (the "Investment Company Act").

Name of General Partner/Investment Manager: The summary also states who is the General Partner and the Investment Manager. If your fund will be managing in excess of $25 million and you are exempt from registering as an adviser in your home state, then you must include that the Investment Manager is not currently registered with the SEC as an investment adviser but is classified as an "exempt reporting advisor" under the U.S. Investment Advisers Act of 1940, as amended (the "Advisers Act"), and, as such, files certain information with the SEC on Form ADV.

Investment Description and Strategy: The summary should contain a brief description of your investment strategy and objectives. Keep this to a few paragraphs since the details will be described within your PPM.

Suitability Requirements: Following the description of your strategy, you will describe your investor suitability requirements. Your hedge fund offering is not registered under the Securities Act of 1933, as amended (the "Act"), as it is being made in reliance on the exemptions provided for in Section 4(2) of the Act and Rule 506 of Regulation D. As the General Partner, you may, in your sole discretion, accept or decline to admit any investor.

Subscription Process: New investors may subscribe for the Interests of your fund typically on the first day of any calendar month or at such other times as you shall permit. Upon completion of the subscription agreement and the receipt of an investor's subscription amount, an investor will become a Limited Partner of your fund.

Transferability of Interests in the Fund: Interests may not be sold, transferred, pledged or assigned without the prior written consent of the General Partner.

Minimum Investment: The minimum initial investment by each investor is described here but it is always subject to your discretion to accept a lesser amount.

Initial Lock-up Period: If you opt to have an initial lock-up period, your investor/Limited Partner may not withdraw capital from your fund for a specified period set by you (typically 6 months to 1 year) following the date of such investor's capital contribution.

Management Fee: As the General Partner/Investment Manager, you will charge your fund an annual management fee (the "Management Fee") of let's say, 1.75% per annum of the net asset value of your fund. One-twelfth of the annual Management Fee would be payable monthly in advance on the first day of each calendar month based on the net asset value on such day (after taking into account any contributions on such day). The Management Fee shall be assessed pro-rata to each Limited Partner within each share class. If a new or existing Partner makes a contribution to the Fund on any day other than the beginning of a month, the General Partner would be entitled to a pro-rated Management Fee at that time. You will also state that the Management Fees are nonrefundable. You certainly have the right to waive all or a part of the Management Fee with respect to one or more Limited Partners from time to time in your sole discretion.

Allocation of Profits and Losses: The profits and losses of your fund will be allocated among the capital accounts of your Investors/Partners (including the General Partner) at the end of each accounting period of your fund in proportion to the relative values of such capital accounts at the beginning of such accounting period.

Carried Interest or Performance Fee: At the end of each fiscal year (or sooner as the case with a BVI fund) of your fund, the Carried Interest/Performance Fee is allocated to the General Partner in an amount equal to what you decide (i.e. 20%) of the aggregate net profits of the fund allocated annually to the all the Limited Partners' Capital Accounts, subject to a "high water mark" limitation, so that no allocation is made to the General Partner with respect to its Carried Interest/Performance Fee until prior net losses allocated to the Limited Partners are recouped.

ERISA and Other Tax Exempted Investors: Since your fund may generate "unrelated business taxable income" within the meaning of the Internal Revenue Code of 1986, as amended (the "Code"), an investment in your fund may not be suitable for pension and other funds subject to the Employee Retirement Income Security Act of 1974, as amended ("ERISA"). It is your responsibility as the General Partner to use commercially reasonable efforts to cause "benefit plan investors" not to own a significant portion of any class of equity interests in your fund, so that the assets of the fund should not be considered "plan assets" for purposes of ERISA and Section 4975 of the Code, although there can be no assurance that no "plan asset" status will be obtained or maintained.

Withdrawals of Capital: A Limited Partner may make withdrawals of capital on 30 days prior written notice to the General Partner at the end of the Initial Lock-Up Period with respect to the Class of Interests for which the withdrawal is desired and at the end of each calendar quarter thereafter. A Limited Partner shall be deemed to have requested the withdrawal of its entire Capital Account if, after giving effect to such withdrawal, the value of the Partner's Capital Account would be less than his initial investment. Distribution of any withdrawal generally will be made within 15 days after the withdrawal date, although 10% of any withdrawal that represents more than 90% of a Limited Partner's capital may be withheld until your fund receives its audited financial statements for the calendar year during which the withdrawal was made. The General Partner may vary these withdrawal terms, in whole or part, for certain investors, in its sole discretion.

Limitations on Withdrawals: The right of any Limited Partner/Investor to withdraw any amount from its Capital Account and to have distributed to it any such amount (or any portion thereof) is subject to the provision by the General Partner for you're your fund's liabilities in accordance with applicable jurisdiction law and for reserves for contingencies and estimated accrued expenses and liabilities. In addition, no withdrawal should be permitted that would result in a Capital Account having a negative balance.

Gate Provision: If withdrawal requests are received in any given quarter which would give rise to aggregate withdrawal proceeds in an amount greater than 20% (this number is used as an example but it is an industry-standard) of the net asset value of your fund as of any Withdrawal Date, you, as the General Partner may at your discretion, satisfy all such withdrawal requests or you may apply what is called a "Gate." This provision would reduce all withdrawal requests *pro rata* so that only withdrawals giving rise to aggregate withdrawal proceeds in an amount up to 20% of the net asset value of the Partnership as of the Withdrawal Date are withdrawn.

Required Withdrawals: You may also, at your sole discretion, require any Partner to withdraw from your fund, with or without cause, if you shall determine, in your sole and absolute discretion that such termination and withdrawal shall be in the best interests of your fund.

Indemnification of General Partner and Investment Manager: The Limited Partnership Agreement provides for limitations on the liability of, and for the indemnification of, the General Partner its affiliates and certain related persons, except that no such indemnification will relieve any person from liability for fraud, gross negligence, willful misconduct, the violation of U.S. federal or state securities laws or any criminal wrongdoing.

Risks: Prospective Investors/Limited Partners should note that an investment in your fund involves a significant amount of risk, including the possibility of a total loss of their investment. Prospective Investors/Limited Partners should carefully consider the risk factors discussed under "Risk Factors" section in your PPM.

Reports to Investors/Partners: Your hedge fund will furnish to each Partner: audited annual financial reports of the fund; annual tax information for the completion of income tax returns; a statement detailing the Partner's capital account; and unaudited periodic reports from time to time at the discretion of the General Partner, but typically no less often than quarterly.

Fiscal Year: The fiscal year of your fund should end on December

31 of each year unless otherwise stated.

Administrator: The name of your administrator is stated here. The Administrator, among other things, administers the fund's affairs on a day-to-day basis in coordination with the General Partner, calculates the profits and losses among the Partners' Capital Accounts as at the end of each accounting period and on such other days as determined by the General Partner; maintains the financial records of the Fund; and processes the subscriptions for Interests and withdrawals in accordance with PPM and the fund's Limited Partnership Agreement.

Directory

Following the Summary is Directory. The Directory located in your PPM consists of all the names and contact details of your service providers to the fund. The following include:

- Registered Office
- Principal Office
- Auditor
- Administrator
- General Partner
- Investment Manager
- Prime Broker
- Bankers and Custodian
- Fund and General Partner Legal Counsel

This is just a shortlist. You may need to add other providers or change as the need arises.

Introduction

The introduction portion consists of the following:

Overview: The overview of your PPM addresses the name of the fund, its address and contact person. It also states that your fund is being operated pursuant to an exemption from registration as an investment company under Section 3(c)(1) of the 1940 Act. As a result, the number of Partners is limited to 100 persons. Otherwise, it can be considered a Section 3(c)(7) fund which would permit institutional investors.

The Management of The Fund: The name of the fund manager. It's credentials and other information that describes how the manager is.

The Offering: This is the portion where you describe your fund offering. Your offering, through your PPM, limited partnership interests to eligible purchasers. Investment in your fund might not be suitable for certain other tax-exempt investors. Only investors who are: "accredited investors" in the meaning of Rule 501 of Regulation D under the Securities Act; "qualified clients," as defined in Rule 205-3 under the Advisers Act; and knowledgeable and experienced in management and business matters such that they are capable of evaluating the merits and risks of an investment in the Fund will be permitted to invest in your fund.

It also states that an "accredited investor" includes natural persons who have a net worth, taken together with the net worth of their spouse, in excess of $1 million (excluding personal residence) or who had individual income of more than $200,000 in each of the prior two calendar years, or joint income with their spouse in excess of $300,000 for each of those years, and who reasonably expect to reach the same income level in the current year; investment partnerships and other entities all of whose equity owners are accredited investors; and entities with assets in excess of $5 million. A "qualified client" includes persons having at least $1,000,000 invested in the Fund or otherwise with the General Partner, or persons having a net worth (together, in the case of a natural person, with assets held jointly with a spouse and exclusive of personal residence) of more than $2,000,000 at the time of their subscription.

ERISA and Other Tax-Exempt Investors: This section addresses that an investment in your fund may not be suitable for pension and other funds subject to the Employee Retirement Income Security Act of 1974, as amended ("ERISA"), or other organizations that are generally exempt from income taxation pursuant to Section 501(c)(3) of the Code.

Allocation of Profits and Losses; Performance Allocation (Carried Interest): As discussed before, the profits and losses of your fund will be provisionally allocated among the capital accounts of the Partners and the General Partner (collectively, the "Partners") at the end of each calendar period in proportion to the relative values of such capital accounts at the beginning of such calendar period.

High Water Mark: The Carried Interest/Performance Fee allocable to the General Partner is subject to a "high water mark" limitation so that no allocation is made to the General Partner with respect to its Carried Interest until prior net losses allocated to a Limited Partner are recouped.

New Partners; Additional Capital Contributions: This paragraph addresses that you, as the General Partner shall allow a new Investor/Partner to be admitted in to your fund, and each existing Investor/Partner may make an additional capital contribution to your fund, as of the first day of a calendar month provided that the General Partner timely receives and accepts such person's initial or additional, as applicable, capital contribution and executed Subscription Documents or such other documents or agreements as the General Partner or Administrator may require.

Withdrawals of Capital; Limitations on Withdrawals: This is a detailed description of the investment capital withdrawals and limitations. Basically, your Limited Partner may make withdrawals of capital on 30 days' prior written notice (or you can decide 60 days) to the General Partner at the end of the relevant Lock-Up Period and at the end of each calendar quarter thereafter.

Lock-Up Period: Your "Lock-Up Period" means with respect to your Limited Partners, a certain period of x months after the date of a Investor/Limited Partner's capital contribution during which such your Investor/Limited Partner may not withdraw any part of such Investor/Limited Partner's capital account related to such capital contribution. I can impose that the Partner pays a withdrawal fee equal to x% (can be from 1 to 5%) of the amount withdrawn.

Fees and Expenses: A detailed breakdown of your fund's expenses and how it shall pay, or reimburse the General Partner for, all reasonable costs and expenses (including the fees and expenses of counsel and accountants) incurred by or on behalf of your fund in connection with the formation and operation of the Fund and the offering and sale of the Interests.

Management Fee: Pursuant to the Limited Fund Agreement, your fund will pay you, General Partner a management fee (the "Management Fee"), monthly in advance, equal to a certain percentage described here (Ex. 0.146% or 1.75% per annum) of the net asset value of the capital accounts of the Limited Partners. The Management Fee shall be assessed pro-rata to each Limited Partner.

Indemnification of the General Partner and Investment Manager: Your fund's Limited partnership agreement provides limitations on the liability of, and for the indemnification of you, the General Partner, its officers, directors, members, employees, agents and representatives, and their respective affiliates, except that no such indemnification will relieve any person from liability for fraud, gross negligence, willful misconduct or any criminal wrongdoing..

Commissions, Etc.: The General Partner may pay (to the extent permitted by law) commissions or other compensation to qualified brokers and other persons who introduce prospective investors to the Fund. The General Partner may waive or reduce its "Carried Interest" requirement with respect to any such person who is an investor in the Fund.

Privacy Policy: Your Subscription Agreement will provide an Exhibit statement addressing your fund's Privacy Policy.

Termination of the Fund: Under normal circumstances, your fund will continue to operate until terminated at the election of the General Partner or otherwise by operation of law.

Investment Activities of the Fund

This section describes your investment strategy and approach. This is also the section where you address your risk management pertaining to operations. Operational risk can be summarized as risk resulting from inadequate or failed procedures, people and systems. Portfolio Risk. Portfolio risk is the possibility that an investment portfolio will fail to meet financial objectives.

Management Company of the Fund

General: It states who is the manager of your fund. Where is it located or domiciled. It also addresses that you, the General Partner, will have exclusive control over day-to-day operations of your fund. It notes who is the principal of the General Partner as well as the principal office.

Principals' Background and Experience: This is where you can brag on your experience, education, and accomplishments. So as long as it relates to you managing your fund. Caution: If you are in the middle of a lawsuit, an investigation, or have had your securities licenses revoked or suspended, you must disclose this (including recent bankruptcy). I do not suggest that you attempt to word this on your own in your PPM. Have your hedge fund consultant and attorney assist in this.

Other Activities: According to your Limited Partnership Agreement, the principals of the General Partner (i.e. You) will devote as much time to the business of your fund as you deem advisable. In addition, the General Partner has the right, without the consent of the Limited Partners, to admit additional managers at the commencement of any calendar quarter or any other time as the General Partner determines. The Limited Partners do not have any right to participate in the management of the Fund and have limited voting rights.

Potential Conflicts of Interest: You, as the General Partner or your principals may be affiliated with or render services to other investment entities or accounts including entities or accounts with investment goals and strategies similar to those of your fund. The principals of the General Partner may also be or become related to other service providers who will provide services to your fund under arrangements in which fees or commissions will be paid to them. These service providers may include broker-dealers, prime brokers or fund administrators.

Limitation of Liability; Indemnification: The General Partner and its directors, officers, employees, agents, servants, delegates and affiliates will not be liable to your fund for any acts or omissions in connection with the services rendered in the absence of gross negligence, willful default or fraud on the part of the General Partner or its directors, officers, employees, agents, servants, delegates or affiliates. In addition, your fund will agree to indemnify the General Partner and its directors, officers, employees, agents, servants, delegates and affiliates from and against any and all liabilities and expenses arising out of the General Partner's actions, other than liabilities and expenses arising out of the gross negligence, willful default or fraud on the part of the General Partner or its directors, officers, employees, agents, servants, delegates or affiliates.

Administrator

Pursuant to your administration agreement between your fund and the Administrator, this section will address the duties of your administrator.

Your administrator will perform administrative, accounting and clerical services to your fund, including: calculating the net asset value of your fund and the profits and losses in each Partner's capital account in accordance with the PPM and the Limited Partnership Agreement; reporting and distributing performance reports and annual financial statements to the Partners; maintaining the financial records of your fund; receiving and processing subscriptions (including AML/KYC due diligence on each prospective investor) for Interests and withdrawals; and performing all other clerical services necessary in connection with the administration of your fund.

For the purpose of calculating each Partner's capital account, your administrator will rely on, and shall not be responsible for the accuracy of, financial data furnished to it by you, the General Partner, brokers or independent third party pricing services. Your administrator will not be responsible or liable for the accuracy of information furnished by other persons in performing its services for your fund. Your administrator in no way acts as an offeror of the Interests, nor is it responsible for the actions of your fund's sales agents, any broker or the General Partner.

Standard Administration Agreements provide that your administrator and its affiliates and agents, their respective officers and employees and their respective successors and assigns shall not be liable to your fund for any error of judgment or mistake of law or for any loss suffered by any of them in connection with the matters to which the Administration Agreement relates, except any loss resulting from the willful or reckless misconduct, bad faith, fraud, or gross negligence of your administrator and its Affiliates in the performance of their duties or material breach of the Administration Agreement. The Administration Agreement also provides that your fund shall indemnify and hold harmless each of your administrator and its Affiliates from and against all expenses, losses, claims, damages or liabilities to any third party, including without limitation any officer, director, partner or creditor of, or any other person having any interest in relation to, your fund, which may arise out of or in connection with the services performed on behalf of your fund under the terms of the Administration Agreement, except any expense, cost, loss, claim, damage or liability resulting from willful or reckless misconduct, bad faith, gross negligence, fraud or material breach of the Administration Agreement on the part of your administrator and its Affiliates in the performance of their duties.

Your administrator's fees are paid out of your fund's assets, having regard to your administrator's standard schedule for providing similar services.

Your Administration Agreement typically can be terminated at any time without penalty by either party usually less than 60 days' written notice, or at any time without such notice in certain circumstances specified therein.

Your administrator shall review and monitor your fund in accordance with the terms as set forth in your Administration Agreement but shall have no obligation to ensure compliance by your fund with the investment policies, restrictions or guidelines applicable to it or any other term or condition of your fund's offering documents. Your administrator is a service provider to your fund and is not responsible for the preparation of your offering documents such as your PPM, Subscription Agreement or the activities of your fund and therefore accepts no responsibility for any information contained in this Memorandum.

Your administrator is authorized to provide information regarding the holding of Interests of each Partner to the General Partner, your fund's legal counsel, and your fund's auditors.

Auditor

The Fund will retain the services of a reputable accounting and advisory firm, experienced in fund accounting, as its independent auditor.

Valuation of the Fund's Assets

The profits and losses of your fund shall be calculated on each fund valuation date (generally the last business day of each month) by your Administrator (in consultation with the General Partner). The profits and losses of your fund shall be determined in accordance with U.S. Generally Accepted Accounting Principles ("U.S. GAAP"), including provisions for accruals and reserves in respect of any amounts constituting your fund's liabilities.

The calculation of the profits and losses of your fund will take into account the total assets of your fund, including all cash and cash equivalents (valued at cost), accrued interest and dividends, and the market value of all securities and all other assets of your fund and all liabilities of your fund including, but not limited to, accrued legal, accounting, and auditing fees, solicitation fees, research-related expenses, operating fees and organizational expenses, and any extraordinary expenses, determined in accordance with U.S. GAAP applied under the accrual basis of accounting by the General Partner in its sole discretion.

Anti-Money Laundering Considerations

As part of your fund's responsibility for the prevention of money laundering, your fund, you, as the General Partner and your Administrator will require a detailed verification of an investor's identity and the source of the payment from any person delivering completed Subscription Agreements to your fund.

In order to comply with proposed regulations aimed at the prevention of money laundering in the United States, your fund is required to verify the identity of all prospective investors and the source of their funds, to the extent required under the USA PATRIOT Act, and to determine if such investors are Prohibited Investors (as defined in your fund's Subscription Documents) identified on various lists maintained by the U.S. Government. If your fund determines that any investor is a Prohibited Investor, your fund may, among other things, freeze that investor's assets in your fund and notify appropriate legal authorities.

Your fund, the General Partner, and your Administrator reserve the right to request such documentation as they deem necessary to verify the identity of a prospective investor and to verify the source of the relevant subscription amounts. The amount of detail required will depend on the circumstances of each application for subscription. By way of example, an individual may be required to produce a copy of a passport or driver's license, together with evidence of his/her address, such as a utility bill or bank statement, and date of birth. For corporate subscribers, your fund may require the production of copies of their certificates of incorporation or other formation documents (and any changes of name) and information concerning their principals or beneficial owners. Failure to provide the necessary evidence may result in subscription applications being rejected or in delays in the processing of withdrawals. Your Subscription Agreement will contain a more detailed description of required anti-money laundering documentation.

If, within a reasonable period of time following a request for verification of identity, the General Partner has not received satisfactory evidence of a subscriber's identity, the General Partner and your fund may, in their absolute discretion, reject the subscription, in which event subscription moneys will be returned without interest to the account from which such moneys were originally debited. Your fund, the General Partner and any agent of your fund and the General Partner will be held harmless and will be fully indemnified by a potential subscriber against any loss arising as a result of a failure to process a subscription or withdrawal request if such information as has been requested by any of them has not been satisfactorily provided by the applicant.

If you have a suspicion that a payment to your fund (by way of subscription or otherwise) or a payment from your fund (by way of withdrawal or otherwise) contains the proceeds of criminal conduct, your fund or the General Partner may report such suspicion to the appropriate authorities. Neither your fund nor the General Partner will incur any liability for adhering to your fund's responsibilities under its anti-money laundering program, and they will be indemnified by the Subscriber for any losses which they or their respective principals, employees or agents may incur for doing so.

Certain Income Tax Considerations

The following discussion is a general summary of certain of the significant United States federal income tax consequences of an investment in your fund. The following discussion does not discuss all the potential tax considerations relevant to your fund or its operations. Moreover, the tax considerations relevant to a specific Partner depend upon such Partner's particular circumstances.

Each prospective Limited Partner is urged to consult such Limited Partner's own tax advisors concerning the potential tax consequences of an investment in your fund.

Other tax considerations address the following:

- Mixed Straddle Election.
- Effect of Straddle Rules on Limited Partners' Securities Positions.
- Limitation on Deductibility of Interest and Short Sale

Expenses.

- Deductibility of Fund Investment Expenditures and Certain Other Expenditures.
- Application of Rules for Income and Losses from Passive Activities.
- Application of Basis and "At-Risk" Limitations on Deductions.

State and Local Taxation: In addition to the U.S. federal income tax consequences described above, prospective investors should consider potential state and local tax consequences of an investment in your fund.

Securities Laws

Securities Act of 1933. The Interests in your fund will not be registered under the Securities Act of 1933, as amended (the "Securities Act"), or any other securities law. The Interests will be offered without registration in reliance upon the exemption contained in Section 4(2) of the Securities Act or regulations of the SEC for transactions not involving a public offering. Each prospective investor must be an accredited investor (as defined in Regulation D promulgated under the Securities Act) and will be required to represent, among other customary private placement representations, that it is acquiring Interests in your fund for investment purposes only and not with a view to resale or distribution.

Investment Company Act of 1940. Your fund will not be registered as an "investment company" under the Investment Company Act in reliance upon Section 3(c)(1). Accordingly, your Investor/Partners will not receive the protections afforded by the Investment Company Act to investors in a registered investment company. Section 3(c)(1) excludes from the definition of investment company any issuer whose outstanding securities are owned exclusively by no more than 100 "accredited investors" (as such term is defined in Regulation D) provided that the issuer is not making, and does not propose to make, a public offering of such securities.

Non-U.S. Securities Laws. The Interests in your fund have not been registered or qualified for public distribution under the securities laws of any jurisdiction. The Interests will be offered without registration and without the filing of a prospectus in reliance upon exemptions available under applicable law. Each prospective investor resident outside the United States must be and will be required to represent that such person is, entitled to acquire Interests in your fund in reliance upon an exemption from the registration or prospectus requirements of applicable securities laws of such person's jurisdiction of residence.

Reports to Partners (Investors)

Your fund will furnish to each Investor/Partner: audited annual financial reports of the Fund; annual tax information for the completion of income tax returns; a statement from your fund's auditors detailing the Investor/Partner's capital account; and unaudited periodic reports issued from time to time at your discretion, but typically no less often than quarterly.

Subscriptions Procedures

To become a Limited Partner, your prospective investor should: complete and execute a copy of the Subscription Agreement, inserting the amount of the capital contribution agreed to be made, the prospective Partner's personal information and taxpayer identification or social security number; provide copies of documents confirming the investors identification, such as a passport or driver's license; and deliver all such documents to your administrator and forward you a copy.

All capital contributions to your fund should be made by wiring cash to your fund's bank account in the name of your fund which should be received at least three business days prior to the subscription date.

In making an investment decision to invest in your fund, your prospective Limited Partners must rely on their own examination of your fund and the terms of your offering, including the merits and significant risks involved. Each prospective Limited Partner should consult their own counsel, accountants, and other professional advisers as to investment, legal, tax and other related matters concerning such proposed investment.

Risk Factors

In this section, you will identify the risk factors associated with your trading strategy and overall fund to your prospective investors. The risk factors below are brief and generic and do not apply to all funds and trading strategies. Many of these risks will be addressed more fully in your completed PPM.

Reliance on the General Partner. The success of your fund depends on the ability of you, as the General Partner/Investment Manager to develop and implement investment strategies to achieve your fund's investment objectives.

Operating Deficits. The expenses of operating your fund could exceed its income. This would require that the difference be paid out of your fund's capital, reducing your funds available for your fund's investments and potential for profitability.

No Operating History. Your fund has no operating or investing history.

Investment Risks. All securities investing and trading activities risk the loss of capital. While you, as the General Partner/Investment Manager will attempt to moderate these risks, there can be no assurance that your fund's investment activities will be successful or that Partners will not suffer losses.

Overall Investment Risk. All securities investments risk the loss of capital. The nature of the securities to be purchased and traded by your fund and the investment techniques and strategies to be employed by the Investment General Partner may increase this risk.

Transactions in Securities. There is no assurance that the Investment Manager will correctly evaluate the nature and magnitude of the various factors that could affect the prospects of the securities in which your fund invests. Your fund may lose its entire investment or may be required to accept cash or securities with a value less than your fund's original investment.

The concentration of Investments. Your fund is not limited with respect to the amount of capital which may be committed to any one investment. Accordingly, your fund may from time to time hold a few, relatively large (in relation to its capital) securities positions, with the result that a loss in any one position could have a more material adverse impact on your fund's capital than would a loss position in a more diversified portfolio.

Leverage. Leverage is the use of borrowed funds for investment. To the extent your fund purchases securities with borrowed funds, its net assets will tend to increase or decrease at a greater rate than if borrowed funds are not used.

Errors in Trading and Trading Strategy. It is possible that the legs of trade entered into by your fund may be input incorrectly due to human error. Your fund intends to employ complex option trading strategies, and accuracy is needed to ensure that all the correct information is entered into the trade screen.

Trading Limitations. For all securities listed on public exchanges, the exchange generally has the right to suspend or limit trading under certain circumstances. Such suspensions or limits could subject your fund to losses.

Portfolio Turnover. Your fund's annual portfolio turnover rate may vary, depending on market conditions, and at times your fund may engage in substantial short-term trading.

Failure of Brokers, Depositories, and External Managers. There is the possibility that the institutions, including brokerage firms, external managers and banks, with which your fund will do business, or with whom securities or cash may be entrusted for custodial or investment management purposes (either in the United States or in foreign countries), will encounter financial difficulties that may result in monetary loss and consequent difficulty in meeting their obligations to your fund.

Transferability and Withdrawal Restrictions. Interests are subject to restrictions with respect to redemption, withdrawal, assignment, and transfer under the Limited Partnership Agreement. Partners may withdraw their capital from your fund at any time following the relevant Lock-Up Period.

Limited Rights of Limited Partners. Limited Partners cannot exercise any management or control functions with respect to your fund's operations, although they have limited rights and duties as set forth in the Limited Partnership Agreement.

Reserves May Affect Withdrawals. You, as the General Partner/Investment Manager may find it necessary, from time to time, to establish a reserve for contingent liabilities. Such reserve would be an asset of your fund but would diminish the amount of capital available to fund withdrawals.

Illiquidity of Interests. The Interests may be acquired for investment purposes only and not with a view to their resale or other distribution.

Limitations on the Obligations of the Principals of the General Partner.

The principals of the General Partner will devote only such time to Fund matters as they, in their sole discretion, deem appropriate.

Risks Associated With the Performance Fee/Carried Interest. The prospect of receiving the Carried Interest could encourage the General Partner to make investments on behalf of your fund that are riskier or more speculative than it would if the General Partner were receiving only a flat fee.

Effect of Substantial Withdrawals. Substantial withdrawals by Partners within a short period of time could require your fund to liquidate positions more rapidly than would otherwise be desirable, possibly reducing the value of your fund's assets or disrupting the Investment Manager's investment strategy.

Potential Mandatory Withdrawal. The General Partner may, in its sole discretion at any time on written notice, require a Limited Partner to withdraw all or a portion of its capital account in your fund. Such mandatory redemption could result in adverse tax or economic consequences to such Partner.

Tax Risks. For a discussion of income tax risks associated with an investment in your fund.

Tax-Exempt Investors; Limitations on Investments. Certain prospective Partners may be subject to U.S. federal and state laws, rules and regulations which may regulate their participation in your fund, or their engaging directly, or indirectly through an investment in your fund, in investment strategies of the types which your fund may utilize from time to time. Each type of exempt organization may be subject to different laws, rules, and regulations, and prospective Limited Partners should consult with their own advisors as to the advisability and tax consequences of an investment in your fund.

SUBSCRIPTION AGREEMENT

The hedge fund subscription agreement is an application or contract to become a member/partner/shareholder investor in a limited partnership or corporation (i.e. Ltd.). The general partner in a limited partnership provides the subscription agreement and requires potential limited partners to complete it. The subscription agreement requires the candidate to divulge financial information relevant to his suitability to invest in the hedge fund. The agreement also states the terms of the partnership/fund.

The subscription agreement contains the following information:

- Subscription Agreement terms
- Accredited Investor Certification.
- Individuals.
- Entities.
- Wire Transfer Page.
- Signature Pages. Complete and sign.

Subscription Agreement Terms and Declarations

Your fund subscription agreement begins by recognizing that your fund, a Delaware limited partnership (for example only), and your Investment manager/General Partner, who is you, will rely on the information set forth, and that the representations and warranties made herein shall be continuing and shall survive the execution of this Subscription Agreement. That each of your Investor/Partners (Subscriber) makes the following statements which shall constitute representations and warranties of that particular Investor/Partner. Your Subscriber will acknowledge the following declarations (declaration statements below is a sample text and can be amended to suit your fund's purpose and strategy):

Application. The Subscriber hereby applies for an Interest in the subscription amount and of the Class set forth below under "Registration Information."

Memorandum. The Subscriber declares that he/she/it has carefully read and understands the information set forth in the Private Placement Memorandum (PPM).

Information Available. The Subscriber confirms that your fund has made available to the Subscriber the opportunity to ask questions of, and receive answers from, your fund concerning the Interests and the terms and conditions of this offering, and to obtain any additional non-proprietary information which your fund has in its possession or was able to acquire without unreasonable effort or expense that was necessary to verify the accuracy of the information in the Memorandum.

Legal Requirements. All legal requirements necessary or appropriate in connection with the purchase of the Interest have been complied with by the Subscriber and each person signing this Subscription Agreement has full legal authority, capacity and power to do so and the Subscriber is not precluded by law, contract or otherwise from purchasing an Interest.

Subscriptions. The Subscriber understands that this subscription, once made, is irrevocable by the Subscriber and that the Administrator will advise the Subscriber as soon as practicable whether this Subscription Agreement, together with all or a portion of the subscription amount, has been accepted or rejected. Subscriptions may be rejected in whole or in part by the General Partner in its sole and absolute discretion.

Payments. The Subscriber understands that any wire transfers sent by your fund to a financial institution pursuant to the Subscriber's instruction will constitute payment to the Subscriber and relieve your fund of any further obligation to the Subscriber with respect to the amounts so paid, and the Subscriber releases your fund from any further obligation with respect thereto.

Reliance on Information Provided. The Subscriber acknowledges that, in deciding to invest in your fund, the Subscriber has relied solely upon the information in the Memorandum.

Securities Act of 1933 and Blue Sky Laws. The Subscriber understands that the offering and sale of Interests are intended to be exempt from registration or qualification under the Securities Act of 1933, as amended (the "1933 Act") and any applicable state or other securities laws and that your fund and the offering of the Interests have not been approved, disapproved, or passed on by any U.S. federal or state agency or commission or by any exchange or other self-regulatory organization.

Investment Company Act of 1940. The Subscriber understands and agrees that your fund is intended to be exempt from registration, and will not register, under the Investment Company Act of 1940, as amended (the "1940 Act").

Disposition. The Subscriber understands and agrees that the Interest may not be offered for sale, sold, pledged, hypothecated, transferred, assigned, or otherwise disposed of (collectively "Disposed of") except as permitted pursuant to the Limited Partnership Agreement, and the Subscriber will not Dispose of or attempt to Dispose of its Interest without the prior written consent of the General Partner, which consent may be granted or withheld in the General Partner's sole and absolute discretion.

Suitability. The Subscriber represents and warrants that (a) the Subscriber meets the suitability requirements set forth in your Private Placement Memorandum.

Fiduciary Capacity. If the Subscriber is purchasing an Interest in a fiduciary capacity, all statements made herein relate to the person or entity for whom the Subscriber is acting.

Information Provided. The information provided by the Subscriber under "Registration Information," the Accredited Investor Certification, Qualified Client Certification, ERISA Questionnaire, and each other required Questionnaire is true and correct and may be relied upon conclusively by your fund and its agents.

Other Documentation. The Subscriber understands that your fund may require other documentation in addition to this Subscription Agreement prior to deciding whether to accept this subscription, and Subscriber agrees to provide it if reasonably requested.

Taxpayer Certification Concerning Status as a U.S. Person. The Subscriber certifies that the information provided and complete in all respects. If the Subscriber is a U.S. citizen or resident and fails to provide the Subscriber's correct Social Security or taxpayer-identification numbers, the Subscriber could be subject to United States withholding tax on a portion of the Subscriber's distributive share of your fund's income.

Fund Status. The Subscriber shall not become a Limited Partner until the Subscriber's name is entered as a Limited Partner on the books and records of your fund.

Appointment of General Partner for Administration Matters. The Subscriber hereby irrevocably constitutes and appoints the General Partner the true and lawful attorney-in-fact of the Subscriber in the Subscriber's name, place and stead, with full power of substitution, to make, execute, sign, acknowledge, swear to, record, deliver and file any of the following documents: the Limited Partnership Agreement and all amendments or restatements of the Limited Partnership Agreement.

Liability. The Subscriber agrees that none of your fund, the General Partner, the Administrator, or any of their respective principals, members, directors, officers or employees shall incur any liability in respect of any action taken upon any information provided to your fund by the Subscriber or for relying on any notice, consent, request, instruction or other instrument believed in good faith to be genuine or to be signed by properly authorized persons on behalf of the Subscriber, including any document transmitted by facsimile or e-mail, or for adhering to applicable anti-money laundering obligations or any other legal requirement whether now or hereinafter in effect.

Indemnification. The Subscriber agrees that it will indemnify and hold harmless your fund, the General Partner, the Administrator and each of their respective principals, members, directors, officers and employees from and against any and all direct and consequential loss, damage, liability, cost or expense (including reasonable attorneys' and accountants' fees, whether incurred in an action between the parties hereto or otherwise) (each, a "Loss") which any of them may incur by reason of or in connection with any misrepresentation made by the Subscriber or the failure by the Subscriber to fulfill any of its covenants or agreements in this Subscription Agreement or in any other document delivered by the Subscriber to your fund.

Anti-Money Laundering. If the Subscriber is an entity (*e.g.*, a corporation, partnership, limited liability company, trust), the Subscriber has exercised due diligence to establish the identity of each person who possesses the power, directly or indirectly, to direct or cause the direction of the Subscriber's management and policies.

Source of Funds. The Subscriber represents and warrants that your funds being used to make this investment is not derived from any unlawful or criminal activities and that the Subscriber has accurately and fully answered all questions directed to the Subscriber, either orally or in writing, with respect to the source of funds being used to make this investment.

Entire Agreement. Your fund's Subscription Agreement and the Limited Partnership Agreement represent the entire agreement of the parties with respect to the subject matter hereof and may not be changed or terminated, except in a writing signed by the Subscriber and the General Partner, or in the case of the Limited Partnership Agreement, in accordance with procedures for amendments as set forth therein.

Accredited Investor Certification

Your Subscriber represents and warrants that he is an Accredited Investor because he states that he is either:

An individual Subscriber who has, or an Individual Retirement Account (IRA) a Keogh Plan covering only a self-employed individual who has, a net worth or joint net worth with that person's spouse at the time of his purchase in excess of $1,000,000 (excluding primary residence).

An individual Subscriber who had, or an IRA or a Keogh Plan covering only a self-employed individual; or a self-directed account of a one-member retirement plan whose beneficial owner had, income in excess of $200,000 in each of the two most recent years or joint income with that person's spouse in excess of $300,000 in each of those years and who reasonably expects income at the same level in the current year.

A corporation, a partnership, or similar business not formed for the specific purpose of making this investment, with total assets in excess of $5,000,000.

An entity in which all of the equity owners are Accredited Investors under Rule 501 of Regulation D under the 1933 Act ("Regulation D").

A trust with total assets in excess of $5,000,000, not formed for the specific purpose of purchasing Interests, the investments of which are directed by a person with knowledge and expertise in financial and business matters, as described in Rule 506(b)(2)(ii) of Regulation D.

A bank, savings and loan association, broker, dealer, insurance company, investment company, business development company, etc.

An employee benefit plan within the meaning of ERISA if the investment decision is made by a Plan fiduciary.

An organization described in Section 501(c)(3) of the Internal Revenue Code, not formed for the specific purpose of making this investment, with total assets in excess of $5,000,000.

Individuals (Questionnaire)

This section of your subscription agreement will consist of a series of questions that your individual subscriber is required to answer. Below is an example of those questions:

1. Name of Subscriber
2. Social Security Number
3. Date of Birth:
4. Occupation:
5. Citizenship:
6. If you are not a U.S. Citizen, are you a permanent U.S. resident?
7. Do you and each other Subscriber (if any) make your own investment decisions?
8. Do you and each other Subscriber (if any) have prior experience in investing in private placements of restricted securities?
9. Does the aggregate investment in the Interests exceed 10% of your and each other Subscriber's (if any) combined net worth (exclusive of home, home furnishings, and automobiles)?
10. Are you or any other Subscriber (if any) subject to any civil, criminal, regulatory or other constraint or are you aware of any impediment or other reason which may preclude or limit your participation in any Fund investment?
11. Is the Interest being purchased as joint tenants?
12. Are you willing to provide additional information, if requested, in order to help the Fund comply with the U.S. Government's anti-terrorism policy as set out in the USA PATRIOT Act?

Entities (Questionnaire)

This section of your subscription agreement will consist of a series of questions that your entity (corporation, partnership) subscriber is required to answer. Below is an example of those questions:

1. Name of Subscriber:
2. Taxpayer EIN Number:
3. Subscriber's Primary Business:
4. Subscriber is (check the appropriate type and provide requested information):

5. Corporation (Date and Place of Incorporation):
6. Limited liability company or partnership (State where formed and date of the organization):
7. Is the Subscriber's principal place of business located in the state of its formation?
8. Is the Subscriber subject to any legal constraints, or is the individual executing this Questionnaire on behalf of the Subscriber aware of any reason which may preclude or limit Subscriber's participation in any potential investment by the Fund?
9. Does the Subscriber have prior experience with private placements of restricted securities?
10. Does this investment constitute over 40% of the Subscriber's assets or committed capital?
11. Was the Subscriber organized for the specific purpose of acquiring an Interest?
12. Do the Subscriber's organizational documents permit the Subscriber to make this investment?
13. Are you prepared to provide the Fund with a copy of the Subscriber's organizational documents upon request?
14. Provide additional information which would be helpful in evaluating the Subscriber's knowledge and experience in financial and business matters:
15. Please describe with particularity the source or sources of the funds used to make this investment:
16. What investment goals do you intend to achieve by investing in the Fund?
17. Are you willing to provide additional information, if requested, in order to help the Fund comply with the U.S. Government's anti-terrorism policy as set out in the USA PATRIOT Act (as defined in Appendix 1)? Are you subscribing, directly or indirectly, for the account of an (a) Prohibited Investor, (b) Senior Foreign Political Figure or (c) member of the Immediate Family or a Close Associate of a Senior Foreign Political Figure (as such terms are defined in Appendix 1)?
18. Is the Subscriber a charitable remainder trust exempt from tax under Section 664 of the Internal Revenue Code?

Wire Transfer Page

This page consists of your fund's wiring instruction. It provides banking details to your subscribers so they can forward it to their banker to expedite the transfer.

Signature Page

This page is self-explanatory.

LIMITED PARTNERSHIP AGREEMENT

Your hedge fund limited partnership agreement outlines the function of the partnership, the duties of you, the General Partner and how the partner's investments are allocated through their capital accounts. Each limited partner has a separate Capital Account for their allocated investment and distribution of profits. The Capital Account is an accounting term used to show how much each investor has invested, any withdrawals made by the investor as well as any distributions to the investor. Each LP has certain amounts of capital contributed by its limited partners. The LP establishes a record for each partner and calls it a Capital Account. The total capital in an LP represents 100 percent of contributions by the partners. Each partner's capital account will reflect his percent investment share in the LP. Net profit or loss will be allocated according to the partnership agreement.

Partners that do not receive a salary have the right to withdraw cash up to the level of there Capital Account balance. If a salary is earned by a partner then that amount is added together and subtracted from any income. Any cash left over would be allocated to each partner. In the case were an LP agreement is not silent, and net profit or loss may be split unequally according to what has been agreed upon in percentages. A partner may put up the same amount of cash as the rest of the partners but may provide other acts of services to the LP. To compensate for the additional services, this partner may receive higher percent distribution yet maintain an equal invested capital interest in the LP.

All U.S. limited partnerships including hedge funds must file a yearly partnership tax return called a Form 1065 with the IRS. In addition to filing 1065, the partnership must provide a K-1 form to all its partners outlining the partner's year-end capital investment, any distributions or losses and remaining capital balances. Partners are responsible to include the figures of their K-1 form when they file their income tax return.

6
CHOOSING THE RIGHT ENTITY STRUCTURE

Typically all types of structured entity provide a degree of liability, tax benefits, and control. Depending on the purpose, it is up to the fund sponsor to decide which entity structure will benefit both the operators of the fund as well as the investors.

Let us first look at the most popular U.S. structures for managing a hedge fund: The Limited Liability Company (LLC) and the Limited Partnership (LP).

Liability

Both the LLC and the limited partnership have one thing in common: limited liability. Liability is of particular importance when the fund manager-member is directly involved with the day-to-day management of the company. With an LLC, liability can be increased or decreased by determining who is running the company. Investors are considered members in an LLC, while the investment manager outside the LLC is hired to manage it. That firm is called a manager; a member may also serve as a manager. An LLC can be composed of managers, members, and member/managers. Managers and member/managers take on the greatest liability since they are involved with the day-to-day management of the company.

In a limited partnership, the limited partners have minimal liability to the extent of their involvement in management. Limited partners are not supposed to be involved with management. It is the general partner's responsibility to operate the partnership in accordance with the limited partnership agreement. Since the general partner is directly involved with managing the company partnership, the liability falls on him.

Unlike a corporation, which pays its own taxes on earned income, a limited partnership, and an LLC both have passed through income or loss features. Every partner or member receives a K-1 form from his respective general partner or manager stating the total earnings minus total expenses and the pro-rata share distribution or loss of the company. Each partner or member then reports his distribution or loss on Schedule E form in his yearly 1040 tax return.

Formalities

The General Partner of a limited partnership is responsible for filing a certificate of limited partnership with the secretary of state in the state where the limited partnership is domiciled. The manager of an LLC is required to file Articles of Organization with the secretary of state in the state in which the LLC is domiciled.

Capital accounts, which identify partners/members contributions and distributions, are required to be current and adjusted for both the limited partnership and LLC.

Filing Costs

Fees vary among states. For example, in Florida, the cost to form an LLC is about $100 for filing and an additional $25 for a certificate designating a registered agent. For a limited partnership, the filing costs are $7.00 per $1,000 of invested capital with a maximum fee of $1,785.

Delaware Limited Partnership

As part of the formation of your hedge fund that will be structured as a limited partnership in Delaware, you must select a name for your fund. The name cannot be the same or related to another company operating within the state unless you receive the written approval of that company. In addition, the name must include the words "Limited Partnership" or "L.P." and must not contain the word "bank" or allude to being in the banking business, unless operating under the supervision of the state bank officials. You may check the availability of any name through the website of the Delaware Department of State, Corporations Division. Once selected, the name may be reserved by filing a name application with the department and including the required fee.

Delaware Formation Process

A Delaware limited partnership hedge fund can be formed by its investors/partners entering into a limited partnership agreement and filing a separate certificate of limited partnership in the Office of the Delaware Secretary of State. A certificate of limited partnership must be signed by all the general partners and state their names and addresses. Your hedge fund limited partnership agreement is not required to be publicly filed or recorded, and the names of the limited partners are not required to be set forth in the certificate of limited partnership. A Delaware limited partnership must maintain a registered agent and a registered office in Delaware.

As the general partner of your hedge fund, you may also be a limited partner, however, the limited partnership must have at least one limited partner who or which must be different from the general partner. Your Limited partners have the same limited liability as a stockholder in a corporation existing under the Delaware General Corporation Law or a member of a Delaware LLC, Sec. 17-303(a).

Delaware Formalities

Standard Delaware formalities state that your Limited partners may not participate in the control of the partnership. If they violate this rule they may become liable as a general partner to persons who transact business with the limited partner and reasonably believe that the person is a general partner. Sec. 17-303(a) has "safe harbor" provisions which permit limited partners to perform defined services for the partnership without becoming general partners. Delaware limited partnerships are formed under the Delaware Revised Uniform Limited Partnership Act, Title 6 Delaware Code §17-101 et seq. (DRULPA).

Your Delaware hedge fund limited partnership is formed by the filing of a "certificate of limited partnership" under Sec. 17-201 of DRULPA. Your Delaware incorporation/registered agent will complete this task for you. The certificate contains the name of the limited partnership, the name, and address of your registered agent and the names and business, or other addresses, of all of the general partners. The hedge fund limited partnership is created at the time of the filling of the initial certificate of limited partnership with the Delaware Secretary of State (Sec. 17-201(b)).

U.S. or Offshore Investors

The question I always ask my clients first when they are deciding on which hedge fund structure is: "Where will your investors be coming from?" If they are coming from the U.S. then it makes practical sense to set up the fund in the U.S. Otherwise, its best to structure the fund in a tax-free offshore jurisdiction such as the British Virgin Islands.

Offshore Fund – Ltd

The British Virgin Islands (BVI) is an attractive jurisdiction for hedge funds. The legislative structure in the BVI is modern and internationally recognized. The authorities have successfully created a framework that is rigorous in terms of anti-money laundering and know-your-customer requirements. It is considerably less expensive to establish a fund in the BVI than comparable jurisdictions such as the Cayman Islands. Hedge funds domiciled in the BVI would benefit from the availability of higher quality banking and custody services in the jurisdiction.

Currently, The British Virgin Islands (BVI) has approximately 3,000 investment funds registered by the BVI Financial Services Commission (FSC). The most popular fund structures are a Closed-ended company (fund) and a licensed Professional Fund.

BVI Closed-end Fund

For emerging managers and traders, a low-cost option to set up an offshore hedge fund is to structure it as a closed-ended investment vehicle. This type of entity does not allow investors to call for redemption of their fund interests or shares. However, there can be language in the offering documents which states that at some point the company (fund) may convert over to a licensed registered fund. This would enable investors to redeem their shares. A closed-end company/fund is simply a company that issues "x" number of shares. This type of company/fund is not required to register with the FSC. It is also important to note that the term "fund" can not be included in the company name. Currently, there are no regulatory rules applicable to closed-ended funds domiciled in the BVI.

BVI Professional Fund

Majority of BVI funds are professional funds. To qualify as a professional fund, fund interests may only be made available to investors who are "professional investors", with the minimum initial investment by each such investor being not less than U.S. $100,000 or its equivalent currency. In addition, the fund sponsors would be required to have an administrator, auditor (optional but recommended), custodian bank and two (2) directors minimum (need not be located in the BVI).

A "professional investor" is defined as a person (i) whose ordinary business involves, whether for its own account or the accounts of others, the acquisition or disposal of property of the same kind as the property, or a substantial part of the property, of the fund; or (b) who has signed a declaration that he, whether individually or jointly with his spouse, has net worth in excess of U.S.$1,000,000 or its equivalent in any other currency, and that he consents to be treated as a professional investor.

FUND STRUCTURE

Your hedge fund consultant and an attorney will walk you through the choices that exist. The first important decision you will make is who you are targeting as investors—people residing in the United States or residents of foreign countries. This decision will impact how your fund is organized.

U.S. fund. For investors residing in the United States, an onshore fund is usually organized as a limited partnership. By purchasing an interest in the partnership, an investor becomes a limited partner of the partnership.

Offshore fund. An offshore fund is organized to make it possible for investors residing outside the United States to invest in your hedge fund. U.S./Offshore funds are typically structured in two ways:

Side-by-side. In a side-by-side structure, US investors typically invest in a limited partnership organized in the United States and offshore investors invest in an offshore corporation. The prime broker typically allocates trade tickets between the domestic fund and the offshore fund.

Master Feeder. This structure allows both investors residing in the United States and investors residing offshore to indirectly invest in the same offshore corporate entity commonly known as the "master fund." Onshore and offshore feeders are used to invest assets in the master fund. The most common U.S./Offshore structure is the Master feeder. See diagram below.

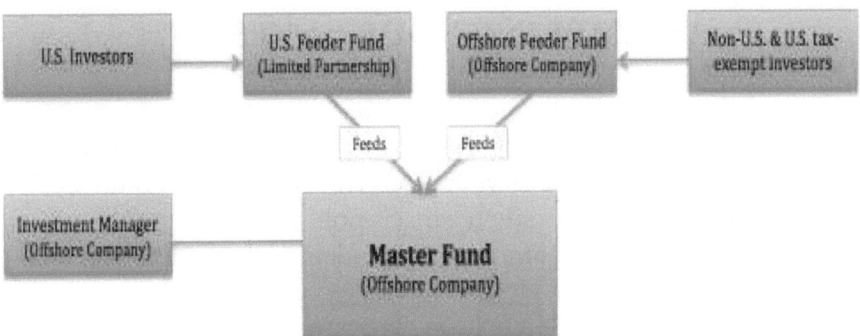

With a Master Feeder structure, your U.S. Feeder Fund (LP) will accept U.S. investors. At that point, the U.S. feeder fund would then subscribe an equal amount of shares/dollars to the Master Fund located offshore (i.e. BVI). Likewise, your Offshore Feeder Fund (i.e. BVI fund) will accept non-U.S. investors. At that point, the Offshore Feeder Fund subscribes and an equal amount of shares/dollars to the Master Fund.

For U.S. tax purposes, the Master Fund located offshore would apply for an entity classification change by filing IRS form 8832 making it into a U.S. limited partnership. This way all net profits/losses will flow back to the U.S. Feeder Fund down to its U.S. investors. There is no adverse effect on non-U.S. investors under this arrangement.

The advantage of having a Master Feeder Fund structure is that you will only need one prime brokerage account to trade out of. The Master Fund will hold that account. Your U.S. and Offshore Feeder funds will have separate subscription/expense accounts to facilitate subscriptions and redemptions as well as paying out your fund expenses.

7
ASSEMBLING YOUR "A" TEAM

After you iron out your initial plans to start your hedge fund, the next step is to select your service providers. Individuals contemplating a hedge fund may not have the established connections with third-party service providers such as administrators, auditors, bankers, etc. However, hedge fund consultants and securities attorneys have pre-existing relationships with one or more service providers, and regularly these service providers can suggest others who may fit well with your new fund. You will be relying heavily on these third parties to meet the needs of your business and partner with you as your hedge fund grows.

There are a number of administrators, auditors, accountants, attorneys, bankers, and prime brokers that want your business. Choosing the right service provider will not only help with the launching process but will benefit you during the operations of your fund.

The cost of bringing on these important players who will be part of your "A" team will greater range to the degree how recognizable they are in the institutional market. If your start-up hedge fund anticipates bringing on investors that will make up $5 million of your fund, then it's possible to choose a smaller, low-cost service provider. Don't be confused with low cost will necessarily equal to low quality of services. This is where you will need to rely on your hedge fund consultant to help with the screening process.

Here are my top two things to consider when choosing your third party service provider:

1. Counterparty risk. A provider's failure to perform can be a result of poor management, fraud or other bad business

practices. When you evaluate your potential service providers, you need to be able to find out the dependability of the continuing service they can provide. This is why many investors of hedge funds will rely on the size and credibility of your service providers.

2. Service Providers who will help you grow. As a start-up fund, you have specific needs. While many of the processes and procedures will continue the same as your fund grows, the level of dealings will likely enhance. As a result, your needs may become more complex over time. Selecting providers that can support you now, as well as in the future, may keep you from outgrowing the services and support they can provide.

Your Attorney

I have personally worked with clients who choose to have their own attorney review and sign off on the fund documents that I prepare. Often times these attorneys are not qualified to review offering documents that relate to U.S. securities laws. Just being familiar with the regulations and rules do not qualify a good securities attorney. I usually recommend one the attorneys that I have worked with in the past. Often times they are much cheaper since I continue to refer them business.

If you opt to use an attorney to draft your offering documents then be prepared to shell out upwards to $25,000. Within their capacity, they are also able to introduce administrators, auditors, and bankers to you and your fund.

Another thing to consider when screening out an attorney is the size of his or her firm. Major Wall Street firms can charge upwards to $75,000 for doing the same work that an attorney of a lesser-known firm that would charge $25k. It's all in the name. So why do some hedge funds pay top dollar to work with these high priced legal gurus? Their investors typically demand it. It goes the same when choosing an administrator, auditor, banker, and prime broker. If you can swing the costs *and* ongoing costs, then it's worth it. BUT, if it sends your fund into the poor house, well, you get the picture.

Your Administrator

Administrators come in all shapes and sizes. The trick is to align yourself with an administrator or "admin" who can best suit your fund's needs – without breaking the bank. Again, if you are targeting institutional investors such as pension funds and family offices then you will most likely decide on a recognizable brand. However, if you have shoestring budget with limited investors (ex. $500k to $5m) then choose a smaller admin shop.

So, for starters, what is a fund administrator? Basically, a hedge fund, administrator serves as an independent third party that protects the interests of investors. The primary function of a third-party administrator is to independently calculate the net asset value of the fund. If the fund manager opts to do this job, it can become a very bias and sometimes fraudulent opportunity to mislead the investors. Remember Madoff?

There are three areas of service which your admin will provide to your hedge fund:

1. Monthly Services

As I said before, the fund administrator primary job is to calculate net asset value of the fund and net asset value (NAV) per share, including full accruals for operating expenses, incentive fees, commissions, and other fees. The industry calls it "striking the NAV." In addition, they prepare and maintain such financial and accounting books and records as are necessary to support an annual independent audit of the fund and cooperate with the auditors.

Other standard services include:

- Provide cash management services for the fund's operating bank account(s)
- Prepare monthly bank account reconciliations
- Create journal entries and post all transactions to a general ledger
- Calculate other income, commissions, and expenses
- Prepare and deliver to the shareholder's final month- end investor statements

2. Middle and Back Office Services

An integral part of the function of an administrator is to maintain a database of all of transactions, open positions, portfolio and account/fund information. This includes:

- Maintain pricing database for historical evaluation and comparison
- Reconcile activity and cash balances monthly
- Report on positions, activity and realized/unrealized gains (P&L) monthly

3. Investor Services and Relations

As a fund manager, you will also pass the responsibility [to your administrator] of maintaining a register of all shareholder information and transactions: receive, review, and process all subscription documents and any requests for redemptions or transfers. Your administrator will also provide KYC/Due diligence services such as:

- Perform anti- money laundering review of all shareholders
- Provide a repository for documents related to the fund
- Assist with annual financial audits and regulatory audits
- Receive and respond to shareholder inquiries

Hiring an experienced hedge fund consultant will greatly reduce the burden of setting up your hedge fund. A good consultant will make the appropriate introductions with the proper service providers that will best suit your needs.

Your Auditor

Auditors also come in all shapes and sizes. However, don't be mislead to believe that all auditors are capable of auditing your hedge fund. When evaluating your potential auditor consider if the firm specializes in auditing hedge funds and other types of investment vehicles. What the size of their staff? How many accountants will be dedicated to your account? In addition to providing your hedge fund with audit services and K-1 preparation for the fund's partners once the fund is launched, your accountants can help you review the initial documents drafted by your lawyer or consultant before they are finalized. In their assessment, they can offer advice on the tax implications related to entity choice and manager compensation. Moreover, if you choose an accountant with hedge fund experience, the accountant should also be able to coordinate with your administrator, prime broker, and internal accounting staff.

Of particular significance and importance is the annual audit, which will be performed by your accountant. Your administrator will work closely with your auditor to ensure that all invoices, payments, credits, brokerage statements, etc. have been properly consolidated. During your fund audit, your accountant will review your financial statements and the capital accounts of the investors (partners) of the fund. As part of this process, your accountant will provide a statement of account to each of the investors, as well as conduct a review of the partnership agreement to determine the partnership percentages.

Your auditor will prepare your hedge fund's financial statements according to GAAP (U.S. General Accepted Accounting Principals) or IFRS (International Financial Reporting Standards) standards. As an offshore fund, your auditor will opt to choose The International Financial Reporting Standards (IFRS) since it is the accounting standard used in more than 110 countries. IFRS has some important differences from the U.S. Generally Accepted Accounting Principles (GAAP). IFRS is considered more of a "principles-based" accounting standard in contrast to GAAP which is considered more "rules-based." By being more "principles-based", IFRS, characterizes and captures the economics of a transaction better than U.S. GAAP. For U.S. funds, relevance, reliability, comparability, and understandability is the key element when utilizing GAAP standards. GAAP establishes a hierarchy of these characteristics. Relevance and reliability are primary qualities. Comparability is secondary. Understandability is treated as a user-specific quality.

Your Banker

In this day and age where money laundering and other white crimes are on the rise, it's important to note that bankers around the world have one eye on sales and the other on scams. In the U.S. there are not many large banks looking to open up bank accounts for investment funds. The reason is that they know that you will be accepting third party funds and investing in various [risky] opportunities. Your banker's number one concern is money laundering. The banker of your choice will evaluate your KYC/AML manual and operations procedures to ensure that you have taken every step to "weed" out any possible threat of illegal activity. From my personal experience, having a general all-purpose KYC/AML manual is important to have for internal purposes. However, the bankers I have worked with do not rely on the fund managers ability (or lack of it) to uncover suspicious activity. Instead, they rely on your administrator. That's right. Your administrator.

As you read previously, one of your admin's job is to conduct KYC/AML procedure on each and every candidate investor. They have the tools and the techniques which enable them to accomplish this very important task. I always recommend that my hedge fund clients rely on their admin's "preferred" banking relationships. The banks that work with your admin have already "approved" them to conduct these procedures when investors have submitted their subscription agreement along with their KYC documents (i.e. passport, utility bill, reference letter).

When you evaluate the bank, be sure that the bank is large enough to take on large investors. If you have a small bank with core capital base is less than $500 million you may have a problem if you have a large institutional investor who decides to invest in your fund in the amount of say, $100 million. However, if you are starting small with anywhere between $1 million to $10 million then I don't see an issue with this. Initially, you will start your relationship with your banker by establishing a basic account. This account will be exclusively for receiving investor funds as well as redemptions, paying out expenses including your management/performance fees, admin fees, and other misc. expenses. Some funds set up two or three sub-accounts for various expense and investment purposes.

It is advised that as the fund manager, you will not have exclusive control over your hedge fund's bank account. Typically, your admin will be a second signor. This assures your investors that you alone will not run away with their money.

Once your investor's funds clear, you and your admin are able to move x dollars to your prime broker where you will have total trading authority. When profits have been realized from your prime brokerage account, you will instruct your prime broker to wire x funds back to your subscription/expense account. Your hedge fund consultant and administrator will guide you through the process.

Your Prime Broker

Prime brokers play an important role when trading all types of securities. Prime brokers (or prime brokerage firms) are securities licensed brokerage firms that specialize in providing bundled packaged services to hedge funds, CTA's, money managers, market makers, and traders who specialize in the private placement market. The main service offered by a prime broker give an investment manager the ability to trade with multiple brokerage firms and liquidity providers while maintaining a centralized location/account at their prime broker. Hence the term "prime broker."

As a one-stop-shop, the prime broker also acts as a settlement agent to the hedge fund and provides global custody of assets such as stocks, bonds, commercial paper as well as MTN's and other financial instruments. In addition, there are also other bundled services which are offered to the hedge fund manager. Some of these include:

- Securities lending – Assets held in custody of the prime broker can be lent out to earn additional fee income to the hedge fund.
- Financing - Credit facilities utilized to leverage the fund's assets.
- Technology – Online/offline software for portfolio reporting needed to effectively manage money.
- Capital Introduction – A service where the prime broker introduces its hedge fund clients to qualified hedge fund investors who have an interest in a particular trading style that the fund trades in.
- Risk Management - Risk analytic technology to help fund manager better handle risks associated with the investments they are trading.
- Prime brokers earn income from "spreads" on financing

the hedge fund's margined long and short cash and security positions, and by charging, in some cases, fees and commissions for clearing and other services.

An Example in a Fixed Income Fund.

For fixed-income or arbitrage funds, the prime broker acts as a settlement agent who facilitates a buy/sell. Only after the end buyer presents a buy ticket/order to the prime, the prime broker would then match the seller of the fixed income security. In this scenario, hedge fund must have sufficient capital with the prime broker to execute the trade. Since fixed income trades settle in T+1 (trade date plus one business day), and the exit buyer/ticket is already in place, it is highly unlikely that the hedge fund would take full delivery of the security And thus, the fund remains in a constant cash position. Prime brokers will earn fee income on settlement as well as any fees earned on the leveraging that may be involved in the transaction.

8
DISASTER RECOVERY & BUSINESS CONTINUITY PLANNING

Nowadays, investors are very diligent in vetting a hedge fund's business and IT procedures. They expect hedge funds and their managers to have comprehensive, detailed plans and procedures in place and often request to see them documented during scheduled, due diligence audits. Moreover, the Securities and Exchange Commission and other state regulatory bodies are becoming more rigorous on disaster recovery and business continuity planning requirements.

For starters, there is a difference between a business continuity plan and a disaster recovery plan. A disaster recovery plan takes into account steps to implement and support the infrastructure (hardware, software, and sites) necessary to make possible the full recovery of services and applications. The steps to access information and applications are addressed in a disaster recovery plan. On the other hand, a business continuity plan makes use of the infrastructure outlined in the disaster recovery plan but focuses on the hedge fund's business operations. It provides answers to questions that are critical to business functionality.

Preparing both a business continuity plan and a disaster recovery plan that will be successful takes time to set up. By completing this process, you and your fund's directors and employees will have an understanding of what processes and procedures are key and will address documenting, planning, implementing, testing and maintaining the policies, procedures and infrastructure to make sure that these crucial procedures can continue to operate and swiftly return to operations after an unforeseen outage.

Your hedge fund should back up all important documents and data offsite in an electronic format at least daily, if not in near-real-time. Developing a system to access critical information and applications in a remote manner will prove useful when an outage occurs by minimizing downtime and enabling the business to maintain operations at close to full capacity. Finally, your hedge fund should be confident enough to test and update both disaster recovery and business continuity plans on a regular basis. This step will assure that when or if the time comes, the business operations will function properly and employees will know how to get the business back up and running efficiently.

Disaster Recovery Planning

Disaster recovery is related to the operations and technology that supports your organization operations. In developing a disaster recovery strategy, your hedge fund will examine what applications and services they have in production and which ones are critical. Electronic files, hard copy files, emails, accounting, and trading applications and telecommunications are often the first that come to mind, but you should evaluate which are most critical of them.

The two most important factors related to disaster recovery planning are the recovery point objective and the recovery time objective.

1. Recovery Point Objective (RPO). The point in time to which hedge fund organization must recover data as defined in advance by the organization
2. Recovery Time Objective (RTO). The duration of time within which a business process must be restored

Business Continuity Planning

A business continuity plan focuses on the development and planning of responding to unexpected events and to address the people, operational processes and business aspects. A hedge fund's business continuity plan should identify the steps necessary to get operations up and running as they relate to business functions and personnel. The business continuity plan is intended to recognize critical services, communications, employee recovery procedures, and training methods.

Typically, there are four business continuity planning steps your hedge fund should follow:

1. Recognize "what" you need to protect. This will help you obtain detailed information about each function's business requirements – both during normal business hours and during a disaster.
2. Decide on "how" you are going to protect. Developing recovery strategies is a great way to plan out your procedures. Identify two or three different scenarios and your corresponding responses. Establish specific communication strategies for each. Be sure to include strategies for both internal and external communications.
3. Instruct key personnel. Set up information sessions with key personnel such as your directors, officers, compliance staff and any other employees so that everyone is on the same page and understands the policies and procedures. Develop resources to distribute, including emergency contact information, wallet cards, and other vital materials.
4. Confirm your plan. Test your alternate site and remote access locations to ensure your business operations will resume quickly and efficiently.

As a new hedge fund organization, it will be necessary to first document your disaster recovery and business continuity procedures before you can begin to fully understand your organizational needs. By starting from the beginning, you will have the advantage to develop your backup procedures at the same time as you develop your normal procedures. By developing your normal and emergency procedures concurrently, you will likely save time and effort in developing your business continuity and disaster recovery plans and the organization will benefit in the long run.

Developing an Operations Manual

Managing the range of the practical aspects of your daily operations and third-party service providers is a necessary, but time-consuming task. As your hedge fund is formed and launched, you will make frequent decisions about your office location, size, functionality as well as the roles and responsibilities of the people working within your hedge fund firm. As you transition from start-up to ongoing management, you will need to redefine your operations. All through this process, you will need to approach your operations as a fund manager and be able to differentiate between serious issues and those that are nice to have but probably are not necessary.

It is advisable to draft an operation manual. Your hedge fund operation manual will govern many of the high-level activities. You will need fully develop policies and procedures for all aspects of your internal operations, from how you communicate with current and potential investors to how you work with your service providers, and from document management to reporting performance.

To create an operations manual, begin by documenting all of the tasks you perform as you complete them. Have this list compiled into a single document and group procedures together. At that point, you can analyze your procedures as they presently are and identify possible areas for improvement. After you refine those areas, you will have a working operations manual that can be shared with others in your organization. Remember to update your operations manual as you expand and grow your firm and add more functions/employees.

9
GET READY TO LAUNCH

Raising Capital

Your new hedge fund's success is heavily reliant on you and your team's capability to raise capital. As a fund manager, you will need enough capital to manage to successfully execute your investment strategy. There are a number of things to consider when developing a plan to attract capital, including the types of investors to target, the resources needed to present your fund and very important regulatory and legal requirements.

Developing a Plan to Attract Investors

The first thing to consider when you are developing a plan to attract investors is to determine what types of investors to approach. Typical hedge fund investors evaluate a number of factors when deciding whether or not to invest in a hedge fund. More importantly, is the fund's manager's investment educational history and previous track record. Since your fund is considered a start-up hedge fund, you will generally target investors who are different from those that are targeted by hedge funds with an established track record. Here is a list of the types of investors you can target:

Seed yourself. If you have no track record but have enough trading experience trading with your own funds then you can contribute or seed the initial capital to launch your fund. Since you are seeding your own fund, you will ask your administrator for a reduced monthly fee until you are able to attract more investors. However, during this time, your admin will log your trades, produce monthly accounting statements as well as calculate your net asset value (NAV). You can opt to waive your performance/management fee as well so that all your capital can be fully utilized for trading. Another thing to consider is that most investors will be more comfortable investing in your fund if they know that you have "skin" in the game.

Seed investors. Seed investors frequently invest at the early stage of a hedge fund's development, including start-up. These are great sources to start with since they have the mindset going in that you and your fund are new and that the fund has no particular track record. Often times these investors might look for certain privileges, such as reduced performance/management fees associated with making the initial investments.

High-net-worth individuals. High-net-worth (or HNW) investors typically invest on an individual basis. This HNW is made up of doctors, lawyers, CPAs, C class executives, professional athletes, and entrepreneurs. According to Wikipedia, in 2012 the United States had over 3.4 million HNW with Japan trailing second at 1.9 million. These HNW individuals usually own four cars or more, have two to three homes worldwide and either owns a yacht or a private jet – sometimes both. Once you have seed capital operating in your fund, especially if part of it is your own money, you will have a good chance with securing a comfort level with these guys – with the anticipation of cutting you a check.

Family offices. Forbes magazine defines a single-family office as an organizational structure that manages the financial and personal affairs of one wealthy family. Because a single-family office is driven purely by the needs and preferences of the underlying family, there is no standard for how one should be structured. Family offices are usually set up as a limited partnership or limited liability company for the exclusive purpose of managing founder's family's wealth. Family offices will normally invest in a blend of both start-up funds and established firms. They are more likely to invest in funds with fewer assets under management, and they tend to look for funds that will provide diversification in their portfolio and have the potential to generate considerable returns. The "gatekeepers" of this investor group is not easy to penetrate. You will need to spend a considerable amount of time building a rapport with this individual. It's all about trust and credibility. Remember, you're not the only fund trying to break into their portfolio. Be patient.

Institutional investors. Institutional investors include pension funds, foundations, endowments, funds-of-funds (FOF), and banks. Institutional investors, especially those that manage money for other individuals, usually have a fiduciary responsibility and are more likely to scrutinize a hedge fund's size and track record. They often look for larger funds that have sizeable assets under management and have had a strong performance record for several consecutive years.

Below is a breakdown of different types of institutional investors:

- **Pension Funds**. A pension fund is any plan or fund which provides retirement income to employees of companies, state and federal institutions. The employee will make certain contributions from their paycheck in which the employer would match or contribute more or less. The funds are placed in a pool with other employees funds in which advisors, trustees, and other investment professionals would then manager with a goal to earn as much of return as possible with limited risk to the principal capital. Pension funds are especially important to the stock market where large institutional investors dominate. The largest 300 pension funds collectively hold about $6 trillion in assets

- **Foundations**. A foundation is a legal entity that operates as a nonprofit organization. Foundations will either donate funds and support to other organizations or provide the source of funding for its own charitable purposes. This type of non-profit organization differs from a private foundation which is typically endowed by an individual or family.

- **Endowments**. An endowment is a fund that has a certain restriction placed on it. Only the interest or profits earned from the fund can be spent, not the principle that supports the endowment. As a rule, only a portion of the interest or earnings from the endowment (typically 5%) is spent on an annual basis in order to assure that the original funds will grow over time. Professional money managers often oversee endowment funds, investing the money in stocks, bonds, and other instruments.

- **Fund of Funds**. The term "fund of funds" (FOF) is an investment fund that holds or owns interests in other hedge funds. A multi-asset FOF will invest in hedge funds that trade commodities and futures, options, equities, bonds. A multi-strategy FOF may invest in other funds with various strategies such as long/short, merger, directional and so on. This type of investing is often referred to as multi-manager investment. A fund of funds may be "fettered", meaning that it invests only in funds managed by the same investment company, or "unfettered", meaning that it can invest in external funds.

Once you decide what types of investors to target, prepare a strategy to successfully market your fund. Your fund can choose to either hire internal staff or retain third-party service providers to promote the fund. If your marketing team will consist of you and your employees then you will generally leverage your network of friends and family and possibly third-party resources, such as prime brokers, to find potential investors. This option may be more practical since you will not have to pay external vendors for marketing support and can have more control over the process.

If you wish to outsource the marketing function then choose firms that specialize in marketing start-up hedge funds to different types of investors. You may choose to outsource the responsibility to experts who focus on this service so you do not have to hire and manage internal staff. However, hiring a third-party marketing firm can be costly and often entails some type of retainer, as well as a potential share of both your management and performance fees.

Another tool to market your hedge fund is to hire a public relations firm to help generate more publicity with the goal of gaining additional credibility in the marketplace and attracting more investment capital.

Marketing Your Fund

As a hedge fund consultant, I am often asked, "What is the best way to market a U.S. hedge fund or offshore hedge fund for raising capital?" The simple answer is there is none. There are many tools and strategies out there to market hedge funds such as online databases, marketing firms, and networking conferences. They all can be very effective in marketing your hedge fund. However, I have additional tips that fund managers can consider and if properly implemented (I mean complying with local regulations), can see results.

Publish a press release. Publish a press release at least six times in a year. Speak to your legal counsel to make sure that what you say is not violating any laws or regulations. There are free press release sites as well as ones that charge for distributions. I suggest that you combine both. The press release firms that do charge are well worth every penny. They have the relationships with Reuters, Bloomberg, AP and Yahoo finance to get your press release to appear in these highly visible sites.

Speak at public events. Speak at public events, conferences, networking events and other places in the industry where you will be heard not only by others in the industry but probably a few members of the press as well. I have assisted my clients to get connected with these global events so that maximize their fund's exposure.

Write a book. Consider writing a book on your experience. Many professionals in the hedge fund industry are often interviewed on TV and online after they have published a book on a specific topic in the hedge fund industry, such as regulation or a specific trading strategy. Do you say that you have never written a book? Join the club. I never thought I would be writing articles or even publishing a book.

Create a pitch book. Create a powerful pitch book through PowerPoint. I suggest that you reserve at least 20% of your PowerPoint presentation to educational content. Underline terms used in the industry and note that definitions are provided at the bottom of the page. Explain your investment process so that anyone institutional or HNW could understand

Market to small wealth managers. Go after small to mid-size wealth management & financial planners. Everyone wants the "big fish". But let's face it, they are dealing with the "big hedge funds".

Approach wealth management firms and financial planning groups that serve HNW professionals from *time to time* but don't manage $1 billion in total assets. You can google or visit the state's regulatory web site to locate RIAs and wealth managers in your area. Just a word of caution. These managers/advisers take time to develop a comfort level with them. It's not always about high profits and trailing commissions (for the properly licensed advisor/planner). It's about relationship and trust.

At a minimum, your marketing strategy should include the following:

- Types of investors
- The amount of capital you are seeking to raise
- Other objectives unique to your fund's strategy
- A detailed marketing plan
- Marketing materials
- All regulatory and legal requirements – *very important*
- Someone who will be responsible for making sure the marketing plan is properly executed
- The hiring of any appropriate third-parties to assist you

Global Fund Exchange www.globalfundexchange.com is an excellent start to market your hedge fund. Another source is Cognito Media www.cognitomedia.com.

Legal Items to Consider

It is crucial that, as a hedge fund manager, you consider regulatory and legal requirements when preparing marketing materials for your hedge fund. There are specific regulations about who a fund can and cannot approach. For example, if you rely on Regulation D rule 506 exemptions from registration, then you will only be catering to accredit investors who earn a minimum of $200,000 per year and have a net worth of $1 million. However, since this is a hedge fund, you will need to also rely on the Investor Advisors Act which states that your investors must either invest a minimum of $1 million into your fund or have a minimum net worth of $2 million. Therefore, it is important to consult with legal counsel when preparing marketing materials for your fund.

Beware of Unlicensed Introducing Agents

The U.S. Securities and Exchange Commission (SEC) is specific when it states (Securities Act of 1934) that no U.S. person can be compensated for referring/introducing capital in a private/public offering unless they are properly licensed (i.e. registered broker-dealer).

If you are looking for capital for your hedge fund, be cautious if individuals who want to earn a percentage fee for introducing capital to you.

According to the SEC, security sold in a transaction that is exempt from registration under the Securities Act of 1933 (the "1933 Act") is not necessarily an "exempted security" under the Exchange Act. For example, a person who sells securities that are exempt from registration under Regulation D of the 1933 Act must nevertheless register as a broker-dealer. In other words, "placement agents" "referring agents" and "introducing agents" are not exempt from broker-dealer registration.

Issuer's "Exemption" and Associated Persons of Issuers (Rule 3a4-1)

Issuers such as the company or hedge fund raising the capital for their own purposes generally are not "brokers" because they sell securities for their own accounts and not for the accounts of others. Moreover, issuers generally are not "dealers" because they do not buy and sell their securities for their own accounts as part of regular business.

Exchange Act Rule 3a4-1 provides that an associated person (or employee) of an issuer (company or hedge fund) who participates in the sale of the issuer's securities would not have to register as a broker-dealer if that person, at the time of participation: (1) is not subject to a "statutory disqualification," as defined in Section 3(a)(39) of the Act; (2) is not compensated by payment of commissions or other remuneration based directly or indirectly on securities transactions; (3) is not an associated person of a broker or dealer; and (4) limits its sales activities as set forth in the rule.

Marketing your Hedge Fund in the European Union

If you intend on marketing your hedge fund to investors located in the European Union (EU), there is another set of rules which need to be adhered to. This pertains to the U.S. or non-EU managers/funds who market to EU investors.

Fund managers who are managing anywhere other than the EU, such as the United States, but are marketing their hedge funds in the EU are subject to certain parts of the directive. Marketing under the directive pertains to the "at the initiative of the manager or on behalf of the manager" among EU investors. This means that those who are engaged in passive marketing, or manage a fund of which the investor initiated the purchase, are not covered by the AIFMD. But a fund manager from the US who uses a placement or distribution agent will be subjected to the directive. These fund managers need to make sure that the EU member states in which they are selling have some sort of private placement regulations (and exemptions) in place and that they may register with the regulators of each of those EU member countries. The AIFMD will not apply to:

- AIFMs managing AIFs that have total assets of less than €100 million (Euros); or
- AIFMs managing AIFs that have total assets of less than €500 million (Euros) subject to the AIFs not being leveraged and have no redemption rights during a period of 5 years following the date of the initial investment in each AIF.

AIFMs located outside the EU who can accept subscriptions from EU investors ONLY if they do not initiate the approach (reverse solicitation/inquiry). Soft Marketing is defined in the Directive as involving an "offer" of units or shares in a fund to prospective investors. "Soft" marketing to investors with early-stage documents cannot technically be an "offer" since there is nothing that can yet be legally accepted. Use general material such as pitch book, slide presentation, etc. should be acceptable provided that you restrict the number of people who receive this material and take back copies that are not absolutely necessary.

A FINAL WORD

I hope that you have found this ultimate hedge fund guidebook to be a practical tool for getting your new hedge fund off the ground. It is only an introduction to the thrilling world of hedge funds, but it can be utilized as a roadmap to help you determine and organize your next steps.

One word of caution. Do not take your investors trust for granted. It is always an extreme privilege for an investor to entrust their capital into your hands to carefully manage. Regrettably, I have seen all to often the downfall of greed and how it affects the ones taken by it. A few past clients are now serving anywhere between 12 to 30 years in federal prison for failing to operate their investment opportunity in accordance with regulatory and ethical standards.

On the other hand, there are many sources and professionals that can help you to remain compliant to state and federal regulations as well as from choosing your structure to marketing and managing your hedge fund. There is no substitute for common sense and gut feeling. With the right advisers, service providers and even investors, and a little luck you will be on the way to forming and managing a successful hedge fund.

GLOSSARY

A

Alpha
A numerical value indicating a manager's risk-adjusted excess rate of return relative to a benchmark. Measures a manager's "value-added" in selecting individual securities, independent of the effect of overall market movements.

Auditor
A certified public accountant who examines a company's books according to a set of procedures and issues a report.

B

Beta
A coefficient measuring a stock's relative volatility to a market index, such as the S&P 500 Index. A manager with a Beta greater than 1.0 is more volatile than the market, while a manager with a Beta less than 1.0 is less volatile than the market.

Bottom-up investing
An approach to investing which seeks to identify well-performing individual securities before considering the impact of economic trends.

C

Capital structure arbitrage
An investment strategy that seeks to exploit pricing inefficiencies in a firm's capital structure. Strategy will entail purchasing the undervalued security, and selling the overvalued, expecting the pricing disparity between the two to close out.

Convertible arbitrage
An investment strategy that seeks to exploit pricing inefficiencies between a convertible bond and the underlying stock. Manager will

typically long the convertible bond and short the underlying stock.

Corporate debt
Non-government-issued interest-bearing or discounted debt instrument that obligates the issuing corporation to pay the bondholder a specified sum of money, at specific intervals, and to repay the principal amount of the loan at maturity.

D

Debt
The general name for bonds, notes, mortgages, and any other forms of paper evidencing amounts owed and payable on specified dates or on-demand.

Distressed securities investing
Investment strategy focusing on troubled or restructuring companies at deep discounts through stocks, fixed income, bank debt or trade claims. Seeks to exploit possible pricing inefficiencies caused by the lack of large institutional investor participation. The approach generally involves a medium- to long-term holding period. Such funds are usually able to achieve low correlations to the broader financial markets.

Diversification
Minimizing of non-systematic portfolio risk by investing assets in several securities and investment categories with low correlation between each other.

Derivative
A financial instrument whose performance is linked to specific security, index or financial instrument. Typically, derivatives are used to transfer risk or negotiate the future sale or delivery of an investment. Derivative instruments come in four basic forms: forward contracts, futures contracts, swaps, and options.

Drawdown
The percentage loss that a fund incurs from its peak net asset value to its lowest value. The maximum drawdown over a significant period is

sometimes employed as a means of measuring the risk of a vehicle. Usually expressed as a percentage decline in net asset value.

E

Emerging markets investing
A generally long-only investment strategy which entails investing in geographic regions that have undeveloped capital markets and exhibit high grow rates and high rates of inflation. Investing in emerging markets can be very volatile, and may also involve currency risk, political risk, and liquidity risk.

Equalization amounts
Distribution to limited partnership interests according to high-water provisions, to properly account for performance-based fees, which may differ among investors, depending on the investor's entry points into a fund.

Equity market neutral investing
Equity investing on both the long and short side, with equal dollar amounts. Will attempt to neutralize market risk, and isolate a manager's alpha, to achieve absolute returns.

European equity hedge
Hedged European equity investing on both the long and short side. Although generally directional in nature, will attempt to hedge out some market risk, and achieve some level of absolute return objectives.

Event-driven investing
Investment strategy seeking to identify and exploit pricing inefficiencies that have been caused by some sort of corporate events, such as a merger, spinoff, distressing situation, or recapitalization.

F

Fixed-income arbitrage
An investment strategy that seeks to exploit pricing inefficiencies in

fixed income securities and their derivative instruments. The typical investment will involve long fixed income security or related instrument that is perceived to be undervalued, and short a similar, related fixed-income security or related instrument.

Fixed income directional
Fixed income investing in the long or short side, based on a manager's view of current market pricing of fixed income securities.

Fund of Funds (FOF)
Investment partnership that invests in a series of other funds. The portfolio will typically diversify across a variety of investment managers, investment strategies, and subcategories. See multi manager

Fundamental investment analysis
Analysis of the balance sheet and income statements of companies, including sales, earnings, growth potential, asset size and quality, indebtedness, management, products, and competition. in order to forecast their future stock price movements.

G

General partner
Managing partner of a limited partnership, who is responsible for the operation of the limited partnership. The general partner's liability is unlimited.

Global macro investing
An investment strategy that seeks to profit by making leveraged bets on anticipated price movements of global stock markets, interest rates, foreign exchange rates, and physical commodities. In this approach a fund manager seeks to anticipate broad trends in the worldwide economy and exploit these.

Government debt
Government or agency-issued interest-bearing/discounted debt instrument that obligates the issuing corporation to pay the bondholder a specified sum of money, at specific intervals, and to

repay the principal amount of the loan at maturity. U.S. government issues are backed by the full faith and credit of the U.S. government, which, if necessary, can print money to make payments.

Growth stocks
Equity of a corporation that has displayed faster-than-average earnings gains over the past few years, and is expected to continue to show high rates of earnings growth. Growth stocks will typically have a higher price/earnings ratio because of their higher expected earnings growth.

H

Hedge fund
A private investment vehicle whose manager receives a significant portion of its compensation from incentive fees tied to the fund's performance -- typically 20% of annual gains over a certain hurdle rate, along with a management fee equal to 2% of assets. The funds, often organized as limited partnerships, typically invest on behalf of high-net-worth individuals and institutions. Their primary objective is often to preserve investors' capital by taking positions whose returns are not closely correlated to those of the broader financial markets. Such vehicles may employ leverage, short sales, a variety of derivatives and other hedging techniques to reduce risk and increase returns. The classic hedge-fund concept, a long/short investment strategy sometimes referred to as the Jones Model, was developed by Alfred Winslow Jones in 1949.

High-water mark
A provision serving to ensure that a fund manager only collects incentive fees on the highest net asset value previously attained at the end of any prior fiscal year - or gains representing actual profits for each investor.

Hurdle rate
The minimum return necessary for a fund manager to start collecting incentive fees. The hurdle is usually tied to a benchmark rate such as Libor or the one-year Treasury bill rate plus a spread.

I

Incentive fee (performance fee)
The charge -- typically 20% -- that a fund manager assesses on gains earned during a given 12-month period.

Inception date
The day on which a fund starts trading; often also expressed as ITD (Inception to date - which illustrates the performance of the fund since its inception)

Investment adviser
Individual or entity who provides investment advice for a fee often called "the manager" see below

Investment manager
Individual who is responsible for the selection and allocation of investment securities.

J

Junk bonds
Corporate bonds with a credit rating of BB or lower. Also known as high yield bonds. Usually issued by companies without long track records of sales or earnings, or by those with questionable credit standing.

L

Leverage
The borrowed money that an investor employs to increase buying power and increase its exposure to an investment. Users of leverage seek to increase their overall invested amounts in hopes that the returns on their positions will exceed their borrowing costs. The extent of a fund's leverage is stated either as a debt-to-equity ratio or as a percentage of the fund's total assets that are funded by debt.

Limited partnership
Many hedge funds are structured as limited partnerships, which are

business organizations managed by one or more general partners who are liable for the fund's debts and obligations. The investors in such a structure are limited partners who do not participate in day-to-day operations and are liable only to the extent of their investments.

Lock-up
The period of time -- often one year -- during which hedge-fund investors are initially prohibited from redeeming their shares. Two kinds of "lock-ups" exist - a hard lock - where the investor is entirely prohibited from redeeming their shares until this period has expired, and a "soft-lock", where the investor can actually redeem, but at a cost. These measures were introduced to discourage short term investing or "hot-money" that would often negatively affect a fund's strategy and performance.

Long-biased investment strategy
An approach was taken by fund managers who tend to hold considerably more long positions than short positions.

Long/short investment strategy
An approach in which fund managers buy stocks whose prices they expect will increase and takes short positions in securities (usually in the same sector) whose prices they believe will decline. The strategy, also known as the Jones Model, is designed to generate profits during bullish periods in the overall stock market while serving as a source of capital protection in a falling stock market.

Large-cap securities
Equity securities with relatively large market capitalization, usually over $5 billion (shares outstanding times price per share).

LDC debt
Debt securities issued by lesser-developed countries.

M

Management company
A firm that, for a management fee, invests pools of capital, for the purpose of fulfilling a sought-after investment objective.

Managed futures
A vehicle in which an investor gives a commodity trading advisor -- usually a manager or broker -- discretion or authority to buy and sell futures contracts, either unconditionally or with restrictions.

Market-neutral investment strategy
An approach that aims to preserve capital through any of several methods and under any market conditions. The most common followers of the market-neutral strategy are funds pursuing a long/short investment strategy. These seek to exploit market discrepancies by purchasing undervalued securities and taking an equal, short position in a different and overvalued security. Market-neutral funds typically employ long-term holding periods and experience moderate volatility.

Market timer
A hedge-fund manager that selects asset allocations in anticipation of movements in the broad market.

Master-feeder fund
A common hedge-fund structure through which a manager sets up two separate vehicles -- one based in the U.S. and an offshore fund that is domiciled outside the U.S. -- which serve as the only investors for non-U.S. fund. The two smaller entities are known as feeder funds, while the large offshore vehicle acts as the master fund. The purpose of such an arrangement is to create a single investment vehicle for both U.S. and non-U.S. investors.

Merger arbitrage investment strategy
Trading the stocks of companies that have announced acquisitions or are the targets of acquisitions. Seeks to exploit deviations of market prices from proposed exchange formulas.

Medium cap securities
Equity securities with a middle-level stock market capitalization. Mid-cap stocks will typically have between $1 billion and $5 billion in total market capitalization (shares outstanding times price per share).

Minimum account size
The minimum initial investment amount an investor must allocate in order to enlist the services of an investment manager, via a separate account, or a limited partnership interest.

Minimum additional investment
Minimum incremental capital allocation allowed to an existing investor.

Money manager
A portfolio/investment manager, the person ultimately responsible for a securities portfolio.

Mortgage-backed security
Pass-Through security that aggregates a pool of mortgage-backed debt obligations. Mortgage-backed securities' principal amounts are usually government-guaranteed; homeowners' principal and interest payments pass from the originating bank or savings and loan through a government agency or investment bank, to investors, net of a loan servicing fee payable to the originator.

Multi-manager
Similar to a fund of funds, where the multi-manager selects complementary allocations to other managers that work in conjunction alongside each other to provide better risk-adjusted returns. Not every multi-manager is a fund of funds whilst every fund of funds is a multi-manager.

Multi-strategy
Investment philosophy allocating investment capital to a variety of investment strategies, although the fund is run by one management company.

N

NAV
Net asset value per share--the market value of a fund share. Equals the closing market value of all securities within a portfolio plus all other assets such as cash, subtracting all liabilities (including fees and

expenses), then dividing the result by the total number of shares outstanding. In terms of corporate valuations, the value of assets fewer liabilities equals net asset value or "book value".

The net rate of return
Percentage appreciation from the prior period, after accounting for all fees and expenses.

New issues
Stock or bond offering being issued to the public for the first time. Also known as "hot issue"

Non-directional
Investment strategy with absolute return objectives, irrespective of market movements.

O

Offshore fund
An investment vehicle that is domiciled outside the U.S. and has no limit on the number of non-U.S. investors it can take on. Although the fund's securities transactions occur on U.S. exchanges and are executed by a U.S. manager or general partner, its administration and audits are conducted offshore -- usually in a tax haven like the Cayman Islands. Because it is administered outside the U.S., non-U.S. investors and such U.S. investors as pension funds and other tax-exempt entities aren't subject to U.S. taxes.

P

Pairs trading
A non-directional relative value investment strategy that seeks to identify two companies with similar characteristics whose equity securities are currently trading at a price relationship that is out of their historical trading range. The investment strategy will entail buying undervalued security while short-selling overvalued security.

PIPEs
Acronym for private investments in public entities. Investments

typically made by funds following Regulation D investment strategy.

Prime broker
A large bank or securities firm that provides various administrative, back-office and financing services to hedge funds and other professional investors. Prime brokers can provide a wide variety of services, including trade reconciliation (clearing and settlement), custody services, risk management, margin financing, securities lending for the purpose of carrying out short sales, record keeping, and investor reporting. A prime brokerage relationship doesn't preclude hedge funds from carrying out trades with other brokers or even employing others as prime brokers. To compete for business, some prime brokers act as incubators for funds, providing office space and services to help new fund managers get off the ground.

Private-equity fund
Entities that buy illiquid stakes in privately held companies, sometimes by participating in leveraged buyouts. Like hedge funds, the vehicles are structured as private investment partnerships in which only qualified investors may participate. Such funds typically charge a management fee of 1.5% to 2.5%, as well as an incentive fee of 25% to 30%. Most private-equity funds employ lock-up periods of five to ten years, longer than those of hedge funds

Private placement
Issues that are exempt from public-registration provisions in the Securities Act of 1933. Hedge fund shares are generally offered as private placements, which are typically offered to only a few investors, rather than the general public. They must meet the following criteria:
The issuer must believe that the buyer is capable of evaluating the risks of the transaction.

Portfolio turnover
The number of times an average portfolio security is replaced during an accounting period, usually a year.

Rate of return
Percentage appreciation in market value for investment security or

security portfolio.

Redemption
Liquidation of interests in an investment fund.

Redemption fee
The fee charged upon a voluntary redemption from an investment vehicle.

Redemption notice period
Required notification period of an intended redemption request. Notification is usually required in writing.

Relative value
A non-directional market-neutral investment strategy that seeks to exploit pricing discrepancies between a pair of related securities. The strategy will entail buying the undervalued security and short-selling the overvalued security.

Risk arbitrage
A relative value investment strategy that seeks to exploit pricing discrepancies in the equity securities of two companies involved in a merger-related transaction. The strategy will entail the purchase of security of the company being acquired, along with a simultaneous sale in the acquiring company.

Regulation D
A provision in the Securities Act of 1933 that allows privately placed transactions to take place without SEC registration and prohibits hedge funds from advertising themselves to the general public. It also outlines which parties qualify as company insiders.

Relative-value investment strategy
A market-neutral investment strategy that seeks to identify investments whose values are attractive, compared to similar securities, when risk, liquidity, and return are taken into account.

Risk arbitrage investment strategy
Purchasing stocks of companies that are likely takeover targets, while

assuming short positions in the would-be acquiring companies. Risk arb players can employ an event-driven investment strategy or merger arbitrage investment strategy, seeking situations such as hostile takeovers, mergers, and leveraged buyouts. Such funds typically experience moderate amounts of volatility.

Risk-free rate
The theoretical return on a risk-free investment, usually a U.S. security like T-bills

S

Sharpe ratio
A numerical value indicating risk-adjusted-performance. Calculated by subtracting the risk-free rate of return from average return, divided by standard deviation of returns.

Short-seller
One who sells a security without owning it, with an obligation to buy the security at a later time, and repay the secured creditor who had lent it for sale. Profits will result if the investor is able to buy it back later at a lower price.

Short-biased investment strategy
An approach that relies on short sales. Such funds tend to hold larger short positions than long positions.

Soft dollars
Credits that can be used to pay for research and other services that brokerage firms provide to hedge funds and other investor clients in return for their business. Those credits are accumulated through soft-dollar brokers, which channel trades to multiple securities brokers.

Sortino ratio
Also called the "upside potential ratio." Similar to the Sharpe ratio, it was developed by the Pension Research Institute to determine the amount of "good" volatility that a fund's investment portfolio possesses -- that is, it seeks to define the amount by which the investment pool's value may increase, based on expected pricing

fluctuations.

Special situations investment strategy
An event-driven investment strategy in which the manager seeks to take advantage of unique corporate situations that provides the potential for investment gains.

Standard deviation
A statistical measure of the degree to which an individual value in the probability distribution tends to vary from the mean of the distribution.

For an investment portfolio, it measures the variation of returns around the portfolios mean-average return. In other words, it expresses an investment's historical volatility. The further the variation from the average return, the higher the standard deviation. Risk does not equal standard deviation and standard deviation does not equal risk.

Small-cap
Securities in which the parent company's total stock market capitalization is less than $1 billion.

Soft commodities
Tropical commodities such as coffee, sugar, and cocoa. In a broader sense may also include grains, oilseeds, cotton, and orange juice. This category usually excludes metals, financial futures, and livestock.

Sovereign debt
Fixed-income security guaranteed by a foreign government.

Spin-off
A form of a corporate divestiture that results in a subsidiary or division becoming an independent company

Statistical arbitrage
Market neutral relative value investment strategy that involves the utilization of a quantitatively based investment methodology that identifies securities or groups of securities that are currently trading at

prices out of their historical range. Will involve longing undervalued security and short selling an overvalued security.

T

Top-down investing
An approach to investing in which an investor first looks at trends in the general economy, and next selects industries and then companies that should benefit from those trends.

Turnarounds
A favorable reversal in the fortunes of a company, a market, or the economy at large. Turnaround specialists seek to exploit market pricing inefficiencies in securities of companies that might be on the verge of a turnaround situation.

U

Unlisted security
A security that is not listed on an organized exchange. Unlisted securities are instead traded in the Over The Counter (OTC) Market.

U.S. equity hedged
Directional, U.S.-oriented investment philosophy that invests in U.S.-exchange-traded securities, on the long and short side. Short exposure is utilized to manage portfolio market risk.

V

Valuation
Placing a value or worth on an asset. For alternative investment portfolios, valuation can be determined by the last market-traded price, or by general partner discretion in the case of illiquid securities, where there is no readily available market-pricing mechanism.

Value investment strategy
An approach that involves purchases of stocks that the manager deems to be priced below their intrinsic values, or are out of favor with the market but are still fundamentally solid. Such funds typically

employ long-term holding periods and experience low volatility.

Venture capital
Money is given to corporate start-ups and other new high-risk enterprises by investors who seek above-average returns and are willing to take illiquid positions.

Volatility
The likelihood that an instrument's value will change over a given period of time, usually measured as beta.

W

Warrant Arbitrage
This combines a blend of traditional option pricing calculations together with practical fine-tuning and extrapolations to identify warrant price anomalies on a volatility basis, or where warrant prices have broken their historic relationships with the underlying stock price. The strategy requires a thorough knowledge of empirical regression and volatility crossover analysis.

Z

Zero-Coupon Bond
A Zero-coupon bond (also known as a discount bond) is a bond bought at a price lower than its face value, with the face value repaid at the time of maturity. It does not make periodic interest payments, or so-called "coupons," hence the term zero-coupon bond. Investors earn interest via the difference between the discounted price of the bond and its par (or redemption) value.

REFERENCES

Bloomberg
Bloomberg connects influential decision makers to a dynamic network of information, people and ideas. Our strength - quickly and accurately delivering data, news, and analytics through innovative technology - is at the core of everything we do. With over 15,500 employees in 192 locations, we deliver business and financial information, news and insight around the world.
www.bloomberg.com

Managed Funds Association
The Managed Funds Association (MFA) represents the global alternative investment industry and its investors by advocating for sound industry practices and public policies that foster efficient, transparent, and fair capital markets.
www.managedfunds.org

U.S. Commodity Futures Trading Commission
The mission of the Commodity Futures Trading Commission (CFTC) is to protect market participants and the public from fraud, manipulation, abusive practices and systemic risk related to derivatives – both futures and swaps – and to foster transparent, open, competitive and financially sound markets.
www.cftc.gov

Global Fund Exchange
Global Fund Exchange Group is a diverse global business entirely focused on providing asset management solutions, services, and products to our global investor base of family offices, sovereign wealth funds, pension and endowment funds, and major wirehouses.
www.globalfundexchange.com

National Futures Association
National Futures Association (NFA) is the self-regulatory organization for the U.S. derivatives industry, including on-exchange traded futures, retail off-exchange foreign currency (forex) and OTC derivatives (swaps).
www.nfa.futures.org

U.S. Securities and Exchange Commission
The mission of the U.S. Securities and Exchange Commission is to protect investors, maintain fair, orderly, and efficient markets, and facilitate capital formation.
www.sec.gov

Eze Castle Integration
Eze Castle Integration is the leading provider of IT solutions and private cloud services to more than 600 alternative investment firms worldwide, including more than 80 firms with $1 billion or more in assets under management. Our Eze Private Cloud is the most widely used hedge fund cloud spanning three continents and supporting over 2,000 users and a petabyte of data.
www.eci.com

INDEX

A

accredited investor 38
Accredited Investor Certification 55
accredited investors 29
additional capital contribution 25
Administrator 37, 68
Advisers With Less Than $150 Million in Assets Under 5
Agreement Terms and Declarations ... 51
Alternative Investments 13
Anti-Money Laundering 54
Anti-Money Laundering Certification Form 29
arbitrage 73
Asset-Backed Securities 17
Attorney 67
Auditor 37, 69
AUM 23

B

Back Office 69
Banker 70
business continuity plan 74
Business Continuity Planning 75
BVI 63

C

capital account 26
Capital Account 58
capital accounts 26
Capital Accounts 37
Capital Introduction 72
Capital Structure Arbitrage 18
carried interest 21
Commodity Trading Advisor 8
Compliance 27
Conflicts of Interest 41

Convertible Arbitrage 18
corporate subscribers 28
Counterparty risk 66
Credit facilities 72

D

Delaware Limited Partnership 61
Directory 37
disaster recovery plan 74
Disaster Recovery Planning 75
Distressed Securities 16
Dodd-Frank Wall Street Reform Act and Consumer Protection Act of 2010 4

E

eligible "purchasers" 29
Emerging Market 14
Emerging Market Debt 14
Emerging Market Equity 14
Employee Retirement Income Security Act of 1974 35
Endowments 80
entity classification 65
Equity Directional 14
Equity Fundamental Market Neutral 16
Equity Market Neutral 15
Equity Statistical Arbitrage 16
ERISA 35, 55
ERISA and Other Tax-Exempt Investors 38
European Union (EU) 11
Event-Driven 16
exempt reporting advisers................... 4
Exemption from Certain Part 4 Requirements Where Participants are "Qualified Eligible Persons 10
Exemption from Certain Part 4 Requirements Where Pool Meets

Certain Trading Criteria. 10
Exemption From Registration as a CPO
.... 10
Exemption from Registration as a CTA
.... 10

F

Family offices.................................. 79
first-in, first-out................................ 27
Fiscal Year 36
Fixed Income 17
Fixed Income Arbitrage 17
Fixed Income Directional................... 17
Fixed Income Relative Value 17
FOREX 8
form 1065 58
Foundations...................................... 80
Fund of Funds 13, 81
FUND STRUCTURE........................ 64

G

GAAP 43
Gate Provision................................. 36
General Partner 20
Global Macro................................... 19

H

hedge fund 13
high watermark 21
High Water Mark 39
High-net-worth individuals................. 79
Hurdle Rate...................................... 21

I

incentive fee..................................... 21
Indemnification 40, 41, 54
individual subscriber......................... 28
Initial Lock-up Period....................... 34
Institutional investors........................ 80
Internal Revenue Code of 1986......... 35
Introduction...................................... 37

Investment Advisers Act of 1940...... 33
Investment Company Act of 1940 ... 46, 52
Investment Risks............................... 48
Investment Styles and Strategies....... 14
Investor Services 69
IRS form 8832 65

K

K-1 58
Know Your Client (KYC)................. 27
KYC/AML 71
KYC/Due diligence........................... 69

L

Liability 60
Limitations on Withdrawals.............. 35
limited liability 20
limited partnership 20
Limited Partnership Agreement . 20, 32, 37
Lock-Up Period.................... 25, 26, 39
Long Biased Equity.......................... 15
Long/Short Equity............................ 15

M

Macro... 19
Managed Futures/CTA 18
Management Company of the Fund ... 40
Management Fee 20, 34, 39
marked-to-market............................. 22
Master feeder 65
Master Feeder 65
Master Fund..................................... 65
Merger Arbitrage 16
mid-sized adviser 5
Mortgage-Backed Arbitrage.............. 18
Multi-Strategy/Multi-Style................. 19

N

National Futures Association 8

Non-U.S. Securities Laws 46

O

Offshore Feeder Fund 65
Operational risk 40
Operations Manual 76
organization costs 24
Other Fees and Expenses 23

P

PATRIOT Act 44
Pension Funds 80
Performance Fee 21, 35
Performance Period 22
Portfolio Risk 40
PPM 32
Prime Broker 37, 72
Privacy Policy 40
Private Placement Memorandum 32
professional funds 64
professional investor 64

Q

qualified client 38
qualified clients 29

R

Raising Capital 78
Recovery Point Objective (RPO) 75
Recovery Time Objective (RTO) 75
Registered Office 37
Regulation D 29, 34, 55
Reports to Investors/Partners 36
Risk Management 72

Risks 36

S

Sarbanes-Oxley Act of 2002: 4
Section 3(c)(1) of the 1940 Act 37
Section 3(c)(7) 37
Securities Act of 1933 .... 3, 33, 46, 52
Securities and Exchange Commission 2
Securities lending 72
Short Biased Equity 15
Side-by-side 64
Soft Marketing 12
State and Local Taxation 46
Subscription 25
Subscription Agreement 32, 50
suspend withdrawal rights 26

T

Tax Exempted Investors 35
The British Virgin Islands 63
The European Union Alternative
   Investment Fund Managers
   Directive (AIFMD) 11
The Investment Advisers Act of 1940 3
The Investment Company Act of 1940 3
The Summary. 37

U

U.S. Commodity Futures Trading
   Commission (CFTC) 10
USA PATRIOT Act 28

V

Venture Capital Funds 5

ABOUT THE AUTHOR

Frank Nagy is Managing Director of Frank Nagy Financial Services. Since 1998, Mr. Nagy has been providing business consulting to project managers, traders, and investment advisers seeking to launch their own hedge fund.

As a former FINRA licensed Registered Representative (Series 7/63), stock and Forex traders, as well as fixed income traders have benefited from Mr. Nagy's experience and knowledge in the securities and fund formation process. In addition to being a hedge fund consultant, Mr. Nagy serves as co-adviser to a number of hedge funds. From his fund managerial experience he greatly reduces the burden of setting up and advising on management of a hedge fund as well as making the appropriate introductions with the proper service providers that will best suit his client's needs. By working alongside experienced securities attorneys, Mr. Nagy has assisted his clients seeking to raise capital by assembling the right fund structure.

For the past thirteen years, Mr. Nagy has served as advisor to various non-profit organizations including the Pinellas County Pregnancy Center. In addition, he currently serves as a Congressional Advisory member to past and present members of the U.S. House of Representatives in his district.

Frank Nagy resides in the Tampa Bay Florida area with his wife and four children.

Made in United States
Troutdale, OR
01/11/2024

16893898R00072